" **A** RIOT IS somebody talking. A riot is a man crying out, **'Listen to me, mister. There's something I've been trying to tell you and you're not
listening.'** "

—Nicholas Johnson,
Federal Communications
Commissioner

RIOTS presents a close look at the strengthening
ranks of the oppressed and the angry. It is their
voices, and the voices of reaction, which will
determine the thrust of American democracy for
future generations. In fifteen selections, many first-
hand accounts, RIOTS focuses on individual uprisings that have occurred recently and throughout
American history—their purpose, their results, and
how to deal with and possibly prevent them.

PROBLEMS OF AMERICAN SOCIETY

Focusing on the urban scene, youth, the individual and his search for a better life, the books in this series probe the most crucial dilemmas of our time.

The Negro in the City
Civil Rights and Civil Liberties
Crime and Juvenile Delinquency
Poverty and the Poor
Air and Water Pollution
The Traffic Jam
The Slums
The Draft
The City as a Community
The Consumer
Drugs
Riots
*City Government
*The People of the City
*Racism
*Hunger

* Forthcoming

ANITA
MONTE
and
GERALD
LEINWAND

RIOTS

WSP
WASHINGTON SQUARE PRESS · NEW YORK

RIOTS

Washington Square Press edition published August, 1970

WSP

L

Published by
Washington Square Press, a division of Simon & Schuster, Inc.,
630 Fifth Avenue, New York, N.Y.

WASHINGTON SQUARE PRESS editions are distributed in the
U.S. by Simon & Schuster, Inc., 630 Fifth Avenue, New
York, N.Y. 10020 and in Canada by Simon & Schuster
of Canada, Ltd., Richmond Hill, Ontario, Canada.

1 2 3 4 5 0 1 0

ACKNOWLEDGMENT

This is one of a series of volumes designed to become text materials for urban schools. For their participation in making this possible the authors wish to thank the authors and publishers who permitted their articles to be reproduced here. We are in debt also, to the many with whom selected portions of the manuscript were discussed. The cooperation of the editorial staff of Washington Square Press was indispensable to the successful completion of the volume. We are deeply grateful to Sharon Kanon, whose mature judgment and experience guided us during the preparation of this book.

Preface

In the opening pages of this volume we are told, "A riot is somebody talking. A riot is a man crying out. 'Listen to me, mister. There's something I've been trying to tell you and you're not listening.' " In all ages and in all societies some men have rioted because others have not listened. Yet if a community is to live at peace with itself a riot is a very expensive way for some to make others listen. It destroys the fabric of society by flouting the laws under which men live. It makes men work at cross purposes when only by working together can the desired reform be achieved. It suggests that men have exhausted the means of communication by which civilized men reason with each other.

In many ways this volume has been the most difficult to write of the *Problems of American Society* series. While one can understand the frustrations that arise during the white heat of the struggle to achieve obvious and overdue reforms, one must necessarily write in a cool, dispassionate environment. Because the act of providing a taxonomy of a riot or an analysis of why riots occur is a rational effort to describe irrational behavior, the very effort itself may drain away the emotional causes that lead to riots and may, in some measure, prejudge the behavior of the rioters. It is hoped that in this volume this has not been the case.

What has been attempted here is to show why riots take place and what can be done to bring about more rational communication among the people of urban America. The readings that follow the introductory essay attempt to show other times and other circumstances in which riots have occurred so that the reader can judge for himself what common factors contribute to riotous behavior. The draft riots in New York City during the Civil War, the labor riots of a generation later, and the riots that have torn American cities in our own time may all be examined for the light they shed on civil disorders. As are the other volumes in this series, this is but a beginning of a study of a complex question. Perhaps by reading this volume the reader will be encouraged to make further inquiry.

G. L.

Contents

Contents

Part One

The Problem and the Challenge

"The growing movement of peaceful mass demonstrations by Negroes is something new in the South, something understandable.... Let Congress heed their rising voices, for they will be heard.**"**

New York Times editorial
Saturday, March 19, 1960

THE black community in Memphis, Tennessee, had come alive to the new leader in their midst. He had a dream and the crowd accepted his challenge. His dream was inspired by a strong, overwhelming belief that white men and black men can find a union of understanding and walk together as brothers.

Later, a muffled shot went unheard by the small group that shared his motel quarters. The man who had molded an army dedicated to passive resistance fell to the ground. Martin Luther King, Jr., was dead.

Black people, long guarded by the spirit and ideas of this soft-spoken man, became enraged. Passive restraint was forgotten and violence spread across the country.

Washington, D. C., the nation's capital, was hit hardest of all. For three days terror reigned. When it was finished, it was clear that blacks had begun a new campaign. This country and the entire world became aware that the quietly contained marches of the past were finished. The black man was hitting back, striking hard at all the injustices he has suffered.

During the long hot summers of the recent past, hundreds of outbreaks have occurred in cities, large and small, across the nation. The news media are

The scream of a curse, the tossing of one rock, and the

filled with reports of riots occurring throughout the cities of the United States—Detroit, Chicago, New York, Cleveland, Los Angeles, Washington, Baltimore, and elsewhere. These reports describe the events, the background of rioters, the causes of riots, the actions of law enforcement agencies, civilian and military, in coping with the rioters, and offer suggestions for more effective ways of quelling riots.

Some of these outbreaks are classified as major, some as serious but not major, and others as minor. Despite these classifications, continued violence, no matter to what degree or intensity, can only lead to disaster. What is wrong? Why did people previously intent on peaceful protest turn to riot?

In 1776, the Declaration of Independence held "all men are created equal." In 1862, Abraham Lin-

(Detroit Free Press, Black Star)

crowd that watches is swept up in the making of a riot.

coln, speaking at Gettysburg, held that the Civil War was being fought over the question of whether a nation so conceived and so dedicated can long endure. The United States Riot Commission Report of 1968 warned, "Our nation is moving toward two societies, one black, one white—separate and unequal."[1] Has the battle for racial equality been lost? Will riots win it? Can riots win it?

What Is a Riot?

In 1806 in the first edition of Noah Webster's dictionary, a riot is defined as: "disorderly behavior, tumult." Later, in his *New Collegiate Dictionary*, the definition was broadened to read: "tumultuous disturbance of the public peace by three or more persons assembled together and acting with a common intent." Funk & Wagnalls *New Standard Dictionary of the English Language* interprets the legal definition[2] as: "a tumultuous disturbance of the public peace by three or more assembled persons, who, in the execution of some private object, so do an act in itself, lawful or unlawful in a manner calculated to terrify the people." Federal Communications Commissioner Nicholas Johnson has said, "A riot is somebody talking. A riot is a man crying out. 'Listen to me, mister. There's something I've been trying to tell you and you're not listening.'"[3] These, then, are some of the definitions given to the word riot. But definitions alone do not tell us what a riot really is.

In order to better understand the nature of riots, let us develop one. Three or more people have assembled. Gradually a larger crowd gathers. An incident occurs that triggers an emotional outburst, perhaps vile language, humiliation, or insult. A heated debate among the group follows. The thread of reason is lost as blind fury engulfs the group. Plans for violence are made and the group, now a mob, sets itself into motion. An object of simmering hatred is selected. The mob, both terrified and causing terror, lawlessly tramples upon such opposition to its conduct that may develop. A riot has thus been born.

Four features common to riots are (1) three or more persons, (2) assembly for the purpose of carrying out some common intent, (3) the use of violence, and (4) the use of terror to threaten public peace. No matter how far we may elaborate on the definition we still find that the most important aspects of riots have not been defined.

The common intent of the rioters' action is ascertained from their conduct. Rioters may shout inflammatory slogans or carry placards on which are written or printed provocative and sometimes vulgar statements. As they move and shout, they become like a stone rolling down the mountainside. Gathering pebbles and rocks along the way, they avalanche through the streets, destroying property—often their own. Cars are overturned and personal injury is commonplace. Their crude arsenal includes Molotov cocktails from discarded whiskey bottles and bits of rag and gasoline. Sticks, stones, and even human feces become part of their weaponry. Snowballing, they lose all sense of what they are doing and even why. Windows are smashed, fires set, and the police or military must be brought into play. Here is force against force, and the result can only breed deeper dislike and distrust. An overzealous policeman caught up in the melee may use unnecessary force against

Does the presence of National Guardsmen deter the rioter or inflame him? (Joe Molnar)

the opposition. A rioter hurls a broken bottle at an officer of the law and opens a gaping wound in his forehead. . . . Riots often end inconclusively. They are put down by police, state troopers, or the National Guard. An uneasy peace descends. The law and the courts are brought into the scene to try to decide who's right, who's wrong, and what punishment is appropriate.

Riots can be either offensive or defensive. In either case rioters must have a common center of attraction. The focal point may be a person or an object. It can be an institution or even a symbol. The appearance of any of these can catapult a restless crowd into a screaming mob that escalates itself into riotous action.

For example, in 1967 Negroes living in Detroit participated in an offensive-type riot. In their own neighborhood they rebelled against local symbols of white American society. Properties in their neighborhood owned by whites became prime targets. The outcome was damage estimated at $45 million.

Who Riots?

What kind of people participate in riots? Because many riots, especially recent ones, have occurred in ghetto areas, it is easy to assume that the rioter is an underprivileged ghetto resident who reacts violently to his poor and socially disorganized surroundings. Some say rioters, looters, and arsonists are persons with psychopathic personalities—persons who hate and who revert to an animal state when enraged. These assumptions are questionable.

"First, violence, rioting and attendant looting are in no sense confined to deprived areas. Outbreaks have occurred in such slumless centers as Nyack,

New York, Fort Lauderdale and Lake Geneva, Florida.

"Second, while most of the participants are members of minority or disenfranchised groups, some of the rioters and looters are white, in instances from well-to-do families.

"Third, while members of the white race are usually the avowed targets of these outbreaks, members of the deprived or minority groups are often the greatest sufferers.

"Finally, large segments of the disenfranchised populations, specifically the Negro, are strongly opposed to such 'direct action' because it is inconsistent with their standards and values."[4]

There is no typical rioter. In general, however, a person's intelligence and level of education have less to do with his participation in a riot than the values by which he lives. Values are ethical ideals upon which people base their decisions. In other words, when a choice has to be made and then acted upon, one's values determine his choice and his action. Values have always differed from group to group within our society. The guidelines for behavior among disadvantaged minorities may differ from the values of the upper middle class. The guidelines for behavior among the leaders of industry and government may differ from the principles of militant groups or from the values of high school and college students. Many accept the prevalent values within a society while others reject them and substitute their own.

From the evidence of the riots that have taken place in the racial ghettos of large cities, a profile of the participants may be drawn. The rioter for the most part was a black teen-ager or young adult between the ages of fifteen and twenty-four. He lived in the city in which he rioted. He was a high school dropout, usually unemployed or employed in menial jobs, that is, unskilled or service jobs. He was male and extremely hostile to whites, as well as to middle-class blacks. It is interesting to note that the Riot Commission found that although the participants were high school dropouts, they were more educated than their nonrioting neighbors. And higher-income Negroes were the counterrioters who urged the rioters to "cool it."

In the riots on the nation's campuses the rioters have been of a different breed. If black, they often feel uncomfortable in the largely middle-class collegiate environment into which they have been thrust. Such immersion often causes cultural shock and numbness to the surrounding community. But when the shock wears off, the reaction is often violent as the blacks seek to substitute their values for those of the college. The latter are thought to be hypocritical, dishonest, and contradictory.

If the collegiate rioter is white, he probably comes from an affluent middle-class or even upper-middle-class family. He, too, however, questions the values by which society lives. He is disturbed by the compromises his parents' generation may have made to make and keep money, enjoy success, and live stylishly. Money, a job, and security are no longer adequate goals. Yet he sees his college forcing him to prefer these goals to others. He is embarrassed by the so-called sins of his parents and teachers. They have not ended either domestic or foreign wars. Poverty remains, as does racism. Above all, the draft and its inequities and an unpopular war in Vietnam hang over their heads. Thus the "Now" generation riots against the "Then" generation. It strikes at the college as the nearest and weakest member of the "establishment" that it wishes to destroy. What will rise in its stead, they know not and appear to care less. Yet they riot to destroy traditional values, giving little thought to what will take the place of those values.

Students for a Democratic Society in *The Work-In Organizers Manual* have expressed their frustrations in this manner:

"Our frustration is shared by millions of others. It comes at a time when living conditions are getting worse for the majority of the American people. The war has taken its toll. . . . Taxes take a greater share of peoples' earnings; . . . necessities cost more. These conditions plus deteriorating schools and hospitals, increased unemployment, particularly among youth, and intensified police persecution are behind the hundreds of rebellions of Black people from Harlem to Watts to Washington, D. C.

". . . We want to combat isolation by learning about workers *from the workers,* not just from newspapers or professors . . . by fighting against white racism, by portraying the troubles of black people as against white people. What do workers think about unions, union leaders, the war, the draft, and ghetto rebellions? . . . . We want to show that among the hundreds of black rebellions, *not one* has attacked a white community. . . ."

Why Riot in the Cities?

In recent years America has suffered from an increase in acts of violence. Some of these are race riots. Some are student riots. They all lead, in varying degrees, to looting, burning, physical injury, and counterviolence. Why have they occurred?

They have occurred for many reasons, most of which are complex and not easily identified. They

Some of the reasons for the fast developing "burn-baby-burn" attitude among young militant blacks can be traced to their homes. This bathroom is not an extreme; it is common in ghetto housing. (Franklynn Peterson, Black Star)

may grow out of the preoccupation of Americans with violence generally. This may be seen in the common acceptance of violence in newspapers and magazines, on the radio, television, and in the movies. Resort to violence in some form—war, riots, bloody conflicts—is shown to be an all-American answer to the nation's problems.

On another level, violence may be regarded as the direct result of the failure of America to guarantee human dignity to all its people. In July 1966 the World Council of Churches, in discussing violence, said:

"We understand the state to be that body which claims the right to a monopoly on the use and control of force. Because it has misused that right so extensively, individuals, groups, and populations in the United States are challenging that right. In the resulting clash there has been an explosion of violence. . . . All available means of persuasion must be used to expose the way in which violence and threat of violence are implicit and explicit in the use of power in American society to the disadvantage of the poor and the oppressed. . . ."[5]

Another group believes that the contemporary swing from nonviolent to riotous action is the best solution to social and economic problems. In 1955–56, to arouse the conscience of the nation over the problems of segregation in housing, discrimination in employment opportunities, inferior schools, seggregation of public accommodations—and in the Southern states, the lack of voting rights for all citizens—Negroes used a nonviolent form of protest. It began under the leadership of Dr. Martin Luther King, Jr., against the local, segregated bus system in Montgomery, Alabama.

Nonviolent protesting included public demonstrations, freedom marches, sit-ins, boycotts, and prayer marches. Participants, both Negro and white, were arrested by the thousands because local law enforcement agencies interpreted the demonstrations as acts of civil disobedience. As a result white resistance to the nonviolent movement erupted into anti-Negro race riots. In part, this reaction was due to the fact that violence and rioting are inherent in nonviolent protests.

In May 1961, a biracial group of student freedom-riders went to Montgomery, Alabama, to protest bus-terminal segregation. Upon their arrival they were met with a large crowd intent on resisting the protest. As a result of the riotous action against the nonviolent movement, the Interstate Commerce Commission outlawed segregation in all trains, buses, and terminal waiting rooms and lunch counters. As demonstrations continued, police resistance intensified. The world watched as Southern police used dogs, electric cattle prods, whips, nightsticks, tear gas, and fire hoses as their answer to peaceful protests. At the same time many white civilians rioted against black demonstrators.

Nonviolent demonstrations continued to be met by violent anti-demonstrations. In Birmingham on May 7, 1963, to stop a demonstration, high-pressure fire hoses and police dogs were used. Twenty-five hundred demonstrators, including Dr. King, were arrested and imprisoned. In protest, about 3,000 Negroes rioted through the business district throwing rocks and bricks, smashing windows, and looting. State troopers, using fire hoses and armored police cars restored order.

Determined to stop the nonviolent demonstrations, white resisters instituted another strategy. Medgar Evers, NAACP secretary for Mississippi,

The South gives its answer to peaceful demands for equality.
(Charles Moore, Black Star)

was murdered in June 1963. Four black children
were killed during the bombing of a Birmingham
church on a Sunday morning in September 1963.
These criminal forms of expression—an expression
of white resistance to the nonviolent movement—
shocked the world. Public outrage caused the passage
of the Civil Rights Act of 1964.

As blacks throughout the South and in ghettos of
the North continued to demand full recognition of
their legal rights, their protests became more violent.
Despite warnings from responsible leaders that rioting would only harm the cause, violent protesting
intensified during the 1960s. During the long hot
summers of the middle and late 1960s outbreak after
outbreak occurred.

As a result President Lyndon B. Johnson issued
an Executive Order on July 29, 1967, establishing

a National Advisory Commission on Civil Disorders. The President declared: "The Commission will investigate the origins of the recent disorders in our cities. It will make recommendations—to me, to the Congress, to the State Governors, and to the Mayors—for measures to prevent or contain such disasters in the future."[6]

The Commission reported in 1968 that the basic causes of the civil disorders of 1967 were:

"Pervasive discrimination and segregation in employment, education and housing, which have resulted in the continuing exclusion of great numbers of Negroes from the benefits of economic progress;

"Black in-migration and white exodus, which have produced the massive and growing concentrations of impoverished Negroes in our major cities, creating a growing crisis of deteriorating facilities and services and unmet human need;

"The Black ghettos where segregation and poverty converge on the young to destroy opportunity and enforce failure. Crime, drug addiction, dependency on welfare and bitterness and resentment against society in general and white society in particular are the result."[7]

Can living be so despairing that a human being is driven to escape by any means available? (Ed Lettau)

Also included were several reasons why the riots took place when they did. These are: disappointment with the concrete gains made as a result of the victories of the Civil Rights Movement, the approval and encouragement of violence as a form of protest directed against the nonviolent protest movement, a growing sense of frustration and powerlessness among slum ghetto residents, the new mood of the Negro youth which rejects submission to the "system," the advocating of violence by some black militants, and a widespread belief among blacks in the existence of police brutality and in a "double standard" of justice and protection, one for Negroes and one for whites.

Violence did not erupt as the result of a single incident. Prior to each riot there had occurred a series of incidents which heightened tension among many of the ghetto residents over a period of weeks or even months. At some point, one incident which may have been routine or trivial took place and the breaking point was reached. Thus, the tension exploded into a riot. On hot summer nights when ghetto youth seek relief from the suffocating heat of the tenements, tempers are on edge and tensions are high. In this atmosphere of heat, poverty, and segregation, a destructive environment is born and cultivated. Such an environment, unfamiliar to most whites and many middle-class Negroes, is a place where life has little meaning.

Why Riot on College Campuses?

Recently violence has spilled over onto our campuses and even into our high schools. Duke University, Howard University, Harvard University, San Francisco College, Brandeis, The City College of New York, and the University of California at Berkeley are only some of the schools where academic life has been disrupted. Here, also, youth was moved to violence.

It is difficult to separate the who of campus riots (see p. 77) from the why. However, the specific issues which seem to have triggered campus riots seem to have a common thread. Urban universities in particular have been accused of keeping their doors closed to black and Puerto Rican students. Many of these universities (Columbia and City College in New York and The University of Chicago) actually border on or are located in ghetto communities. Yet they often seem isolated and remote and—worse—indifferent to ghetto needs. Often, too, the very growth of a university seems to be made at the expense of the community, as in the case of Columbia's effort to build a new gym or City's effort to build new classrooms. Whites and blacks here find a common cause to riot.

Other issues causing riots grow out of dissatisfaction with the "relevance" of courses to student needs. Students demand a voice in campus governance. They seek an opportunity to determine the curriculum, hire and fire instructors, and, in the traditions of the old medieval student guild, govern themselves.

Dissatisfaction over the Vietnam war raises a host of issues which encourage riots. Thus, colleges are accused of engaging in secret research that aids the war effort. Or, they permit the military and companies manufacturing war-related products to recruit employees from among the school's seniors. Students do not wish the colleges to give draft boards data about grades or class standing. They want the university to openly oppose war. These issues have kindled riots on nearly every major campus in the nation.

There seems to be a definite thread that links ghetto violence with school violence. In the past black students on campus were politically inactive. As the number of black students increased and the Black Power movement became more influential, black students began to identify with the grievances of the larger black community. In other words, the new mood of ghetto blacks—self-esteem, racial pride, and a search for identity—is shared by the black college students, many of whom are from a middle-class background. The black middle-class students are not necessarily less radical than the ghetto blacks.

The National Commission on the Causes and Prevention of Violence suggests that "the militant stance of some black students may be a major factor in increasing the militance of white students, whose commitments to social justice and equality have been greeted with skepticism by blacks. At Columbia, for example, the white student seizure of some campus buildings [see p. 84] may have resulted in part from openly expressed doubts by black students that the whites were really not prepared to do what both groups felt was necessary to challenge the university and resist the police."[8]

There is a distinct racial pattern to the school conflicts. The black students' demands—black history, more black teachers, more participation in student affairs—are limited in scope. "The white left radicals, on the other hand, see the university as the architect of the power structure—which is the engine of a corrupt society—and want to bring the university down."[9] Black students want to become a part of the establishment, not to destroy it. It is believed by some that the spread of violent action by students—the seizure of principals' offices, scuf-

Campus disorders: Police form a barrier during a student protest demonstration at the University of Wisconsin. The Violence Commission said such demonstrations elevate "physical confrontation over rational discourse." (Ira Block, Pix)

fling between teachers and students, students and students, property destruction, arson, strikes—and the appearance of police on campus and in the high schools is a new manifestation of the polarization of our nation into two camps, one white, one black.

Such confrontations are not only a threat to campus and school life, they are a threat to the surrounding community. For example, in 1968 dissident students at Columbia attacked the university as racist and threatened to enlist militants from the nearby community of Harlem.

Are Riots Planned?

The recent increase in violence in the ghettos, on campuses, and in high schools compels the question: To what extent are riots organized or part of a conspiracy? There is evidence that the growing rebellion of students against teachers, students against students, whites and blacks against each other, ghetto residents against local symbols of white American authority is not usually the result of a spontaneous action.

On the surface rioting may appear to erupt unexpectedly. However, while it develops out of a social atmosphere in which tension-building incidents have occurred over a period of weeks or months or years, riots are usually led if not always planned. While riots can be, and often are, started by an organized group which believes that a riot would be to its advantage, the end of the riot is by no means so predictable.

The amount of planning prior to a riot is not easily discernible. However, incidents such as the repeated gun battles between the Black Panthers and the police and a shoot-out in Cleveland (see p. 162) lead some observers to the conclusion that riots are not spontaneous flareups and some are planned in advance.

However, not all those who participate in the riots have knowledge of the plan. They may be victims of mob psychology practiced on them by a small but forceful minority. To the extent that not all participants are instigators of the riot, the outcome of such conflicts cannot be predicted or controlled.

The United States Riot Commission Report states: "Only a handful realize that Negro accommodation to the pattern of prejudice in American culture has been but one side of the coin—for as slaves and free men, Negroes have protested against oppression and persistently sought equality in American society."[10]

With regard to riots in black urban ghettos, we forget that blacks have often had to resort to violence to break the chains that have tied them to

(Benedict J. Fernandez)

slavery and oppression. As far back as 1712 slave revolts took place. In 1820 Denmark Vesey planned a slave revolt in Charleston but as the plot was uncovered, his plans were fruitless. In 1831 Nat Turner planned and led a bloody rebellion in which 55 whites were killed. Turner's band of some 60 slaves were eventually captured and Turner and 16 of his fellow rioters were later hanged.

Since the days of slave revolts, blacks have protested in a variety of organized ways—from petitions to Congress and Presidents to nonviolent demonstrations and finally to armed uprisings. There have always been leaders who attempted to direct the protest, violent or nonviolent.

In 1909–10 the National Association for the Advancement of Colored People was formed. The NAACP urged legal action in courts and legislatures to protest segregation and to seek the vote for Negroes. Vigorous lawful and nonviolent methods were chosen by the NAACP to win for blacks a secure place in American life.

In 1911 social workers founded the National Urban League which sought a solution to the "Negro problem" through economics. To find jobs for Negro migrants to the cities, the Urban League appealed to the self-interest and conscience of the white businessman.

Interspersed with Negro nonviolent protest was white violent reaction. The most violent occurred in New York City during the draft riots, July 1863. White workers felt they had the most to lose from participation in the Civil War. Also, they were afraid that freeing the slaves would flood the Northern market with cheap labor (see p. 106).

The Ku Klux Klan in the beginning of the late nineteenth and early twentieth century began a campaign to preserve the "supremacy" of the white race. Lynchings, burnings, and floggings were directed against Negroes in Texas, Chicago, Pennsylvania, Washington, D. C., Oklahoma, and elsewhere.

Tired of the slow progress toward gaining equal rights, the black protest movement took a more aggressive turn. A. Philip Randolph was among those who advocated a more radical approach. In 1942 he said, ". . . if Negroes secure their goals, immediate and remote, they must win them and to win them they must fight, sacrifice, suffer, go to jail and, if need be, die for them. These rights will not be given. They must be taken."[11] He called not only for physical resistance but united planned action of the urban working classes, black and white, against capitalists to achieve social justice.

As white terrorism—the murder and abuse of civil rights workers in the South, the offenses by white policemen, and open defiance of the law by officials—seemed to be encouraged, a qualitative shift took place in the 1960s. Emphasis changed from legal action to direct confrontations. Activities of the Student Nonviolent Coordinating Committee (SNCC), started in April 1960, were encouraged by adult participation of the Southern Christian Leadership Conference (SCLC). From 1960 through 1963 the protest movement remained nonviolent. Even though it was met with violence from the police and white mobs, blacks continued to protest quietly in a dignified demonstration of courage and determination.

By 1964 the voices of younger and more militant civil rights organizations were being heard. Deacons for Defense and Justice was organized to give adequate protection to civil rights workers against night riders in the South. The Black Power slogan, which

Demonstrations protest arrest of Black Panthers after recent shoot-outs between the Panthers and police in Chicago and Los Angeles. Panther members charge the United States with genocide. (Julio Mitchel)

means pride and identity to some and violence and separatism to others, was gaining importance. Groups such as the Black Panthers and the Blackstone Raiders trained themselves for armed warfare.

The Black Panthers in their October 1966 platform said, "We will protect ourselves from the force and violence of the racist police and the racist military, by whatever means necessary. We believe we can end police brutality in our black community by organizing black self-defense groups that are dedicated to defending our black community from racist police oppression and brutality."

In 1964 Malcolm X, spokesman of the Black Muslim movement, formed a new movement called the Organization of Afro-American Unity. His followers were told to meet violence with violence.

Although these more militant organizations were unable to enlist the support of the greater majority of

black people, their policies were indicative of the
anger, frustration, and powerlessness felt by all ghetto blacks. Repeated appeals to the Federal Government through the years to help end unemployment,
poor housing, inferior schooling, segregation, and
the increasing white backlash, in addition to a call
for violence by militant organizations and individual
agitators, created an atmosphere of frustration that
boiled over into riots. Thus, we had a state of mind
receptive to violence, a state of mind in which the
blacks no longer believed in the good faith of white
America.

During this period some students, black and white,
were also disturbed by what they felt were gaps between society's stated ideals and society's performance. Students for a Democratic Society (SDS) and
other student groups have often deliberately sought
and planned confrontations with the establishment
(government, colleges, military, and so forth.) To do
this they have practiced jeering at police and "going
limp" when about to be carried off to jail. Some
have even learned the art of judo and karate in
order, as they say, to protect themselves from the
police. In their use of violence and in their response
to violence they have sought inspirational and prac-
tical guidance from the writings of Mao Tse-tung
and Che Guevara. Without leadership from a band
of a few extremist students bent on violence, it is
doubtful that campus riots would have reached current levels. Some of this leadership seems to come
from nonstudents, who have taken it upon themselves
to stir up discord where and when they can.

The Violence Panel, in an appraisal of student
unrest, has said: "The problem of campus unrest is
more than a campus problem. Its roots lie deep in
the larger society. There is no single cause, no single

solution. Students . . . see afresh the injustices that remain unremedied. . . . They see the university, guardian of man's knowledge and source of his new ideas, as an engine for powering the reform of the larger society. . . ."[12]

How Effective Are Riots?

Some groups believe that riots may call attention to conditions requiring change and may lead to remedial actions such as investigations and legislation. *Psychology Today,* a monthly magazine, conducted a poll among better-educated, younger, and high-income whites and Negroes. "The majority believed that riots have positive, long-term effects in changing slum conditions. Sixty-two percent of the respondents were less than thirty-four years old; 82 percent were under forty-four; 76 percent were college graduates; 39 percent have master's, Ph.D.s or other advanced degrees; 46 percent earn more than $10,000 a year. . . . The magazine cautioned [that] this profile of attitudes on urban and racial issues is not that of the general American public. . . ."[13]

Others believe that riots definitely change conditions. Dick Gregory has said, "After Detroit literally burned to the ground, the Ford Motor Company hired 6,000 Negroes in two days' time." (See p. 68.)

On the other hand the casualties and damages inflicted on humans and property and the perpetuation of mutual distrust between the races increases rather than decreases tensions after riots.

"A survey by the Department of Housing and Urban Development found that little had been done to clean up or restore areas damaged by rioting and vandalism in Negro sections a year or more ago."[14]

In Washington, D. C., the rioting that followed the

Washington, D. C. One year later. (OEO)

murder of Dr. Martin Luther King, Jr., created a new slum. Rows of stores that were looted and burned still stand wrecked and charred. In the Hough district of Cleveland, ruins remain four years after the 1966 riots. There are still gaping holes, boarded buildings, and empty lots in the riot areas of Los Angeles.

Throughout the nation job discrimination still forces the minorities into low-paying, low-status occupations. Poverty is still a pervasive fact of life. Ghetto schools are still inferior although some progress has been made. A Federal fair-housing law was passed, but not enough money has been appropriated for its enforcement. The model cities program is limited by lack of funds and now this program in no way appears to be the solution to the death of slums.

Can Riots Be Prevented?

Democracy guarantees the right to dissent. But how this right is to be expressed is one of the most serious problems facing our nation today. Rioting is a violent method of expressing dissent.

Counterviolence or a call for law and order without justice is advocated by some as a means to prevent riots. A call for law and order without justice is approved violence in defiance of the laws of the United States.

For example, at the 1968 Democratic Convention hundreds of demonstrators were injured, over 600 persons were arrested, and more than twenty newsmen accused the Chicago police of unlawful assault. The Walker Report in submitting its findings to The National Commission on the Causes and Prevention of Violence said: "During the week of the Democratic National Convention, the Chicago police were the targets of mounting provocation by both word and act. . . . Some of these acts had been planned; others were spontaneous or were themselves provoked by police action. Furthermore, the police had been put on edge by widely published threats of attempts to disrupt both the city and the Convention.

"This was the nature of the provocation. The nature of the response was unrestrained and indiscriminate police violence on many occasions, particularly at night.

"That violence was made all the more shocking by the fact that it was often inflicted upon persons who had broken no law, disobeyed no order, made no threat. These included peaceful demonstrators, onlookers, and large numbers of residents who were simply passing through, or happened to live in the area where confrontations were occurring.

"Newsmen and photographers were singled out for assault, and their equipment deliberately damaged. Fundamental police training was ignored; and officers, when on the scene, were often unable to control their men. . . . [B]ut Mayor Daley['s] . . . widely disseminated 'shoot to kill arsonists and shoot to maim looters' order undoubtedly had an effect."[15] (See p. 180.)

Today's rioters may be arrested on charges of disturbing the peace and disorderly conduct. When the police charge a group with unlawful assembly and order them to disperse, refusal by any individual to do so means he can be arrested and charged with unlawful assembly. According to the law, an individual who joins a group at any time during a disturbance is subject to arrest. Rioting is a misdemeanor punishable by fine or imprisonment. If armed, the penalties are more severe. To control student violence, a Federal law enacted in 1968 says, "any student convicted of a crime or regarded to have seriously violated college regulations, may be declared by college authorities ineligible for two years to receive Federal scholarships or loans. . . . Colorado has enacted a law which imposes fines of $500 and jail sentences of a year for those who interfere with the normal function of a college or university."[16]

Advocates of suppressive techniques believe a "decline" in large-scale violence is the result of improved police methods, better training of National Guardsmen and troops, and the enactment of severe penalties.

On the other hand suppressive techniques may inflame unrest. The appearance of police on campuses has caused an increase in the intensity of student demonstrations which have often erupted into riots.

There is a call for better ways to solve the dilemma facing our nation. There are programs and new ideas to close the gap between promise and performance. These programs undertake to suggest new beginnings to change the system of failure and frustration that dominates the lives of ghetto residents and divides our country.

Such public aid programs would improve the education, living, and employment conditions of the deprived. They would include:

(1) an open housing law to cover the sale or rental of single family homes;

(2) the location of more low- and moderate-income housing outside ghetto areas;

(3) the creation of an ownership supplement plan so low-income families can own homes;

(4) provision of more social services through neighborhood centers;

(5) the creation of new jobs to absorb the hard-core unemployed;

(6) the removal of artificial barriers to jobs, such as arrest records or the lack of a high school diploma;

(7) the elimination of segregation in schools;

(8) the extension of a quality early childhood education to every disadvantaged child;

(9) elimination of illiteracy through greater Federal support of adult basic education;

(10) assurance of more per-student aid to areas with a high proportion of disadvantaged school-age children.

Riots reflect the failure of state, Federal, and school leadership to solve the dilemma of our cities. They also reflect the failure of the larger part of society to meet the needs of the black community. Today, although some progress has been made in dealing with slum life, there still remains a wide gulf between promise and fulfillment. If the prevailing environment is allowed to continue, conspiratorial violence, riots in the ghettos and on campus, police brutality, white backlash, and black rioting will flourish.

"Only when blacks are competent performers in much more significant numbers with access to every area and level of human endeavor within the society will the impression of white power, superiority, and independence, and black powerlessness, inferiority, and dependence be destroyed. One alternative now is to attempt to achieve these ends within the society, as part of the society and through methods deemed acceptable by the society. Another, most likely to develop if white resistance to full black participation persists, is to move against society—violently. Logic

Peoples bonded together in their search for an alternate to

or concern for the consequences cannot stay passion generated by the desire to satisfy basic human needs. . . . [E]very group . . . must make it clear through rapid and enlightened action that manhood, respect, adequacy, and security are possible within this society or black and white conflict and violence will become more malignant."[17]

We do have alternatives to rioting. Effective substitutes are peaceful demonstrations, labor strikes, mediation, arbitration, organized boycotts, protest, and propaganda. Dissent can be expressed by the written word, by the vote, and on radio and television. These are useful weapons of dissent and they are within the scope of the law. Our Constitution protects the right of all citizens to protest and dissent.

violence. (E. Luttenberg)

It protects the right to assemble and stage mass demonstrations if these activities are peaceable. Peaceful demonstrations impress upon the public and the authorities the issue at hand and they effect changes within the law.

People opposed to the war in Vietnam and to draft policies used the peaceful weapons of dissent to alter the course of the war and the Draft Act. A most remarkable example was the Moratorium protests held across the nation in November 1969. This was the largest protest movement ever seen in this country. Dissenters held no public offices, owned no radio or television stations. They were not publishers of newspapers or magazines. Yet, through the use of peaceful weapons of dissent they effectively presented their beliefs to the public and the authorities. Together they fasted, sang, exercised their right to use the written and spoken word to reach the minds and conscience of the nation. They talked to others about the immorality and senselessness of the war. The Moratorium showed more vividly and dramatically than any other protest tactic how effective these alternatives to violence are.

Part Two

Selected Readings

This pictorial essay describes what happened when twenty million people in our nation are denied the rights and opportunities to which they are entitled. What effect do you think their method of dissent has on the future of our nation?

1

Phases of Dissent

In the beginning there was this . . .

Leonard Freed, Magnum

Leonard Freed, Magnum

and this . . .

Leonard Freed, Magnum

Ernest Baxter, Black Star

Inhumanity made these scenes commonplace.

As the bell of injustice rang loudly the people peacefully

followed Martin Luther King and his impossible dream.

Bruce Davidson, Magnum

In 1949 Congress called for "a decent home and suitable environment for every American family." Two decades later 47 percent of the dwellings occupied by nonwhites are substandard and 24 percent are overcrowded.

And Congress said: "Integrate with all speed." Yet in 1969 we find classrooms like this scattered throughout the South.

Bruce Davidson, Magnum

The eventual changing pattern in the black man's life
brought about his new attitude.

Alan Mercer

Joe Molnar

Kay Kreighbaum, Black Star

He became militant,

Burt Glinn, Magnum

and the riots began.

In this selection Paul Jacobs explores the
causes of the August 1965 riot in Watts
in Los Angeles: the relationship between
the police and the minority population;
the attitudes of social workers; housing;
educational facilities for minorities. Although this is about Los Angeles, do you
believe that it is pertinent to your city?

2

Prelude to Riot

by PAUL JACOBS

. . . [W]HEN the young Negro spat in my face in
downtown Los Angeles, he was spitting on all of
white America. I was Whitey, and he hates Whitey
because he believes Whitey despises and hates him.

And he is right. The pattern of life of poor whites
in America is determined by the contempt in which
they are held for having failed to achieve the individual affluence which is the society's basic value. The

From *Prelude to Riot* by Paul Jacobs (New York: Vintage
Books, 1968), pp. 6–12. Copyright © 1968, 1969, by Paul Jacobs.
Reprinted with permission of Random House, Inc.

life of poor Puerto Ricans, Mexicans, and Indians is marked by the same contempt, mixed with some fear about their odd behavior, the kind of fear that resulted in the infamous "zoot-suit" riots in Los Angeles during the war, when gangs of servicemen roamed the streets, savagely beating every teen-ager who looked like a Mexican. But the lives of the poor Negroes in American cities are marked not only by contempt and fear but by active hate. And it is hate which makes ghettoization continue and intensify.

Another characteristic of life common to all the poor but qualitatively different for minorities is their continual contact with government agencies. . . .

. . . [T]he poor—white, Mexican, Puerto Rican, Indian, and Negro alike—are in continual contact with government agencies. They spend a large proportion of their time waiting for interviews in welfare offices or answering caseworkers' questions in their homes; when they are sick, they wait in the county clinic to see a doctor; they go to a state employment agency for jobs. Because their children frequently get into trouble at school, they are visited by truant officers. Their children get into more trouble outside of school too, and they have more contact with the police, then the courts, then the jails, then the probation and parole officers, and then the police again, as the whole cycle repeats itself. They see the marshals, too, very often when they stop making payments on the TV and the credit store tries to repossess the set. Their cars are old, they have more accidents in them, and they get more traffic tickets which they cannot pay; so they end up being arrested rather than just cited. If they need psychiatric help, they must be committed to state hospitals, unlike those with higher incomes who can remain at home while undergoing treatment.

For most of the poor, then, government is seen as a network of agencies that affect their lives directly and often. . . .

The poor, and especially the minority poor, generally tend, in their contacts with city, county, state, and federal government agencies, to be treated either punitively or in ways which reinforce their feelings of dependency, and frequently both. The help extended to the poor is grudging, tight-lipped, and censorious, for it is generally assumed that they are responsible for their own bad condition and that if they wanted to get out of it badly enough, they could do so.

It is also assumed that they are incapable of running their own lives and that therefore they need not be given the same rights as the rest of society. They are thought of as being somehow subhuman, not truly men and women. That is why the looting and the burning and the sniping take place: a man squinting down the sights of a rifle, hidden from view behind a curtained window, feels powerful, for now he can decide on life or death. A man hurling a Molotov cocktail into a supermarket and watching it burst into flames can say, as one said to me, "That was the first time in my life I ever felt like a man." Another man, who proudly showed me a closetful of suits, said, "Those are loot suits."

And it doesn't matter if the suits don't fit, for they are important as symbols. Looting in the cities can be just as much an act of politics as it is a desire for goods. It is a way in which the poor can make a representation to the society, for they have no other kind of representation; it is a way in which the black poor can express their hate of the white world for not giving them their chance to share in the goodies. And it doesn't matter whether the store being looted is owned by a black man or a white man; *owning* a store is what white people do, not black ones.

The ideas of law and order held by the minority poor can be different from those held by the rest of society. The poor guard their possessions as best they can, but they view the theft of them as being an inevitable part of the world in which they live, rather than as an abnormal circumstance, which is how stealing is perceived outside the ghettos.

So, too, whether or not it is only Jewish men who come to the doors of the poor Negroes selling cheap, shoddy merchandise at high prices, all of them are thought of as Jews, as "Goldbergs in Their Jew Canoes," the Cadillacs in which it is believed they drive into the ghetto to collect the money of the poor. The ghetto dwellers believe it is in the natural order of things for them to be cheated by the Jewish merchants, since they believe cheating to be part of the Jewish psyche. And so, when a "selective demolition program," as the burnings are described, breaks out, the Jewish-owned stores become immediate targets.

But Negro businessmen exploit Negroes viciously, too, and there are Mexican-Americans fattening on the troubles of their community. The ghettos have their own ministers, too, who thrive while their flocks starve (a Cadillac is also called a "Baptist preacher" in the ghetto), their cynical politicians who exploit their ethnic or racial background but do nothing for their constituents, and their "community leaders" seeking only to advance themselves rather than the people they claim to serve. As many organizational jealousies can be found in the ghettos as outside them, and as many groups fighting desperately for the right to speak in the name of the whole community.

So we must learn, painfully, not to romanticize any group and not to expect that a group that is discriminated against is therefore less capable of prejudice against other groups. We must learn how complex are the problems of the urban poor, who have fewer resources to deal with their difficulties than any other group in society. Take health, for example. A family with a pregnant wife, an unemployed sick husband, and two children, one of whom is ill, must get to four different physical locations at four different times in order to even try to solve their health problems: the pregnant mother goes to a prenatal clinic, which meets only twice a week; she takes one child to a Well Baby clinic, which is held on a different day, and the sick child to another clinic, which also meets on a different day; the unemployed father must visit the county hospital for treatment of his illness. In each of these places the waiting time will be interminable; and the family may have to pay for the treatment and care they get.

Or consider what is required to help one unemployed, unskilled Negro teen-ager get a job and keep it: he will probably need a basic education that includes learning how to read, write, and speak intelligibly; his past arrest record will need to be expunged or ignored; he will need many hours of vocational counseling; his poor health will need repairing, some of his bad and rotting teeth replacement; he should spend hours with a psychiatric social worker, and another worker may need to spend hours or days with his family. When all this and a good deal more has been done to help him in his personal life, he will probably still be living in a ghetto from which he cannot escape and be part of a social condition which itself requires fundamental and radical transformation. . . .

This is not to suggest that the ghettos are always frightening, for they are not. Fun and games can be found in them, and there are great sources of humor and deep springs of strength among the ghetto people. . . .

In some important ways the ghettos even give strength and security to the people who live in them, and they are a source of great inner vitality. But this strength, security, and vitality can also be a source of weakness, for it makes the ghetto dwellers want to remain inside the ghetto rather than venture beyond its borders.

Until recently another consequence of remaining inside the ghetto has been that some of its inhabitants, especially the kids and teen-agers, always live part of their lives in a fantasy world. School dropouts, unable to face the reality of working in a car wash, talk about becoming jet pilots. They dream about the hi-fi they will buy when they become wealthy entertainers, for their psyches cannot stand the knowledge that they will be poor all their lives. In their minds the boys see themselves as sexual giants, the girls as sought-after beauty queens. Their transistor radios are turned on all the time to the Negro or Spanish stations; the radio is their fix, the music the drug that takes them out of the ugly reality into a private fantasy world. And if the talk and the radio fail them, they can always light up a joint—for to "blow grass," smoke marijuana, helps greatly to soften the sharp outlines of their lives.

It is hard for such ghetto children to grow up, for they think they have nothing to grow up to, and few of the usual ways in which children become adults are open to them. They do not graduate from high school and then take their first steps toward adulthood and maturity in college or in a job. They

The sweetness of youth has the bitter taste of nightshade for many ghetto youths. (Paul Conklin, OEO)

have no adult occupations with which to identify, and so they remain caught in the matrix of childhood. . . .

These people, adults by chronology but not personality, never have an opportunity to break with the patterns they have learned: to lie to and run from the agencies of government, which they see only in negative and oppressive roles. Their lives run by a clock that keeps C.P.T., Colored People's Time, which assumes that appointments made won't be kept, work promised won't be delivered, jobs found won't be gone to, since those are all part of the outside world. Like Mexican Time and the onetime J.P.T., Jewish People's Time, C.P.T. is a phrase that draws the lines of the ghetto.

. . .

FURTHER INQUIRY

1. How do you account for the attitude of government agencies toward the poor? What could be done to change this attitude?
2. Do you agree with the statement: "Looting in cities can be just as much an act of politics as it is a desire for goods"? Give your reasons.
3. What are the most important causes of riots? How would you go about eliminating these causes?

In 1968 Dick Gregory, comedian and author, ran for President of the United States as a write-in candidate. The selection below, part of his political platform, is his analysis of the Kerner report which states that white racism is a major cause of rioting. What connection is there between racism and rioting? Is it fair to blame white racism only?

3

The Gregory Report on Civil Disorders

by DICK GREGORY

Political Agitators and Ghetto Revolutionaries

THOUGH the Kerner report placed the major burden of blame for rioting on white racism, I hold the politicians primarily responsible. Politicians are more to blame than the average white citizen because they

From *Write me in!* by Dick Gregory and edited by James R. McGraw (New York: Bantam Books, Inc., 1968), pp. 80, 89–96. Copyright © 1968 by Dick Gregory. Reprinted by permission of Bantam Books, Inc., New York, N.Y.

have raised their hand and sworn an oath to uphold the Constitution of the United States. The Constitution gives a man the right to call me "nigger." That is freedom of speech. Freedom of expression under the Constitution gives a citizen the right to both hate me and verbalize that hatred. But no man has the constitutional right to place structural limitations upon my freedom. A man does not have to like me to work by my side, or in my employ or to be my next-door neighbor. But he does *not* have the right to limit my opportunities for employment or my choice of housing.

Politicians in this country have been more concerned with maintaining the positive public opinion of the white electorate than they have with upholding their oath to implement the Constitution. They are making a fatal mistake and must be held personally responsible for the continuation and spread of rioting. The temper of our time demands that political actions be determined by considering how they will affect black folks rather than white folks. It is black reaction which will determine national survival. White folks are not going to burn this country to the ground. The average white man cannot possibly be as bitter as the average black man. The white man has a better job and cannot afford to go to jail. He has much more to lose by participating in civil disobedience or open rebellion in the streets.

The ghetto brother whose anger and frustration has driven him to rebellion does not fear jail. He knows that life in the jail-house cannot be any worse than his present condition. In many ways it is better. The jail is warm, three meals a day are provided, and when the brother comes out of confinement, he is a hero back in his own neighborhood. In a very real sense he is regarded as a freedom fighter and he enjoys a dignity and respect never before accorded him in his life. It is the attitude and potential reaction of just such a man which should concern politicians.

It is this unknown man in the ghetto who is the real threat to national survival. He is strangely faceless, unknown both to the white power structure and to the militant black spokesmen. The government has become so preoccupied with the more vocal representatives of black militance—Rap Brown, Stokely Carmichael, or Dick Gregory—that it has failed to see this invisible man in the ghetto. . . .

The Detroit revolt was a good illustration. When Detroit first began to burn in 1967, every identifiable militant black spokesman in the country was in Newark, New Jersey, attending a conference on Black Power. If Detroit had been a premeditated matter, planned and perpetrated by Black Power leadership, the leaders would have been in the area guiding and directing the action. . . . And America should realize that the very Black Power leaders it vilifies are the true patriots. They are openly articulating a warning to America of impending doom. They are giving a voice to that invisible ghetto presence which will one day act to make the warning a reality. America must heed the warning of her black patriots or suffer the consequences. Whatever the reaction, the nation cannot say it was taken by surprise.

The ghetto revolts up to the present moment have been the result of spontaneous reaction to a triggering incident—an open expression of police mistreatment usually or, more recently, outraged response to the assassination of Martin Luther King. Notice the pattern of ghetto revolt thus far. When the National Guard left the ghetto area, nobody else came in to fan the fires of revolution. If the current ghetto revolts

If each of your days began and ended in a slum with the rats, garbage, debris, crime, addiction, and poverty, you might well end up in jail for rioting. (J. Bruce Baumann, Black Star)

were other than spontaneous outbreaks, that is, the work of outside Black Power agitators, such persons would have moved into action as soon as the Guardsmen left the area.

.   .   .

But the climate is ripe for a shift from revolt to revolution. People who have been arrested and jailed in past ghetto revolts are beginning to come out of confinement. Many such persons were imprisoned for something they did not do. In their anger, cops swept whole street corners clean and grabbed the innocent with the guilty. These persons have been political prisoners and during their imprisonment they have developed an attitude.

Imagine a man who went out into the street during a ghetto uprising looking for his kids. He is a respected father and has a decent job. He found his kids cheering the street activity. And before he has a chance to get his kids back home, the cops arrest him along with the mob. The man is not really worried because he knows that he is innocent and expects to be released when the record is set straight. Then he finds a $50,000 bail placed upon him and hears false charges read against him. He faces an all-white jury which is more inclined to believe the testimony of the police than his own true story. He ends up with a year or two in jail and he knows his only crime was being black.

A political prisoner spends his time in jail seething with resentment. He is determined to get even with the unjust system which has confined him: This determination is the only thing which keeps him going while he is in jail. It is no accident that the great revolutionaries of history have all been political prisoners. A long period of confinement provides the opportunity to plan revolutionary action. The initial anger turns to shrewd calculation. The political prisoner develops a cool attitude, a more long-range view of the total struggle and a realization that change need not be immediate. He sees the futility of spontaneous outbreak and plans a determined strategy for revolutionary action.

.   .   .

Calculated Revolution

. . . Calculated revolution uses the unique natural resources which nature provides to give power to the powerless. For example, it takes only one man to place dynamite in a New York City movie theater. Suppose that happens one day and *The New York Times* gets word that a Loew's theater will blow up in ten minutes. The dynamite is discovered in time to save the theater, but word is circulated that this action was merely one of many planned throughout the country. Do you suppose white folks will be going to the movies after that? Such calculated use of extremely limited resources could be powerful enough to bring the movie industry to a halt.

Or suppose one light-complexioned black revolutionary wanted to set off a spontaneous revolt but needed a triggering incident. All he would have to do is put on a policeman's uniform and go out into the street and beat up a little black kid. Then get in a car and pull away. Everyone would think it was a white cop, the triggering incident would be provided, and block after block would begin to burn. Such is the relative ease with which a disciplined and committed revolutionary can influence the national scene.

When shrewd calculation moves in to replace spontaneous reaction, white America cannot take comfort in relying upon "responsible" Negro leadership to stop revolutionary activity. There is an ethical principle involved. When the nonviolent marches were taking place and peaceful protesters marched singing "We Shall Overcome," the militant revolutionaries did not knock the picket signs out of their hands and replace them with guns. Even though they disagreed with the nonviolent strategy, the militants respected the right of freedom-loving people to demonstrate in their own way. Nor can the nonviolent leaders be expected to knock the machine guns from the hands of revolutionaries and replace them with picket signs. The same respect for a person's right to choose his own strategy of protest must be shown.

Rather than trying to silence the Rap Browns and the Stokely Carmichaels, white America should really be worrying about the day when the voice of warning is silent. Though white racism assumes that black people have a low degree of intelligence, we are not so stupid that we will stand on a soap box and tell you when we are actually going to burn the country to the ground. When the natural haircuts begin to disappear and everyone starts wearing conventional clothes once again, it will be a good indication that the real revolution is at hand. It is the man who blends in with the conventional American scene who is really able to strike by surprise.

Cancel the Flight

Civil disorder in America can be condensed in a simple illustration. Black people in America look at this country as they do a cigarette machine. They just can't communicate with it. Recall your feelings when you are running through the airport, just ready to board your plane, and you stop by the cigarette machine. You put your money in the machine, pull the lever, and no cigarettes fall down. Isn't that a frustrating feeling? Especially when you realize you can't talk to the machine.

Then you pull the change return lever and you don't get your money back. Suddenly you start doing little funny things with yourself. You tell yourself, "I didn't want Winston anyway, I wanted Viceroy." You pull the Viceroy lever and still no cigarettes. So you start pulling other levers. Finally when you have pulled them all, you realize you are not going to get anything for the money you have invested.

So you run over to the ticket counter and explain your problem. The man at the ticket counter says, "Look, I just write tickets for TWA. I can't help you. But there is a message written on the machine that tells you what to do." So you run back and read the message: "In case of problems with this machine, write to Giddings Jones, Kansas City, Missouri." Now you hear the last call for your flight and you stand there looking at that cigarette machine that you can't relate with and that has your money—and your flight is leaving! So you do the normal thing. In a final act of desperation, you kick the machine hard. You don't get your money back but you see the dent in that machine and you feel better.

But imagine your reaction if, after you had kicked the machine and turned away, a big foot came out and kicked you back. If that happened you would cancel your flight, take that machine and tear it up into little pieces, screw by screw.

Black people have invested their money, their lives, their labor, their faith and their trust in America for three hundred years. And we have received nothing for our investment. We took our problem to those who we thought would do something about it.

We even went the long route and wrote to Kansas City in the form of nonviolent civil rights demonstrations. Still no refund.

So in the form of Watts, Newark and Detroit we kicked the American machine, trying desperately to get the attention of the nation. And in the form of the police, the National Guard, and even federal troops, the machine kicked back. Our desperation is now complete. We are saying to this country, "Cancel the flight." And we are going to dismantle this American machine piece by piece.

FURTHER INQUIRY

1. Do you agree with the author's statement that "politicians . . . must be held personally responsible for the continuation and spread of rioting"? Why?

2. Why should the average black man be more bitter than the average white man?

3. If you were a politician, what actions would you take to stop riots?

4. The author calls the Black Power leaders patriots instead of agitators. Do you agree? Give your reasons.

5. Why does the author call the disorders "revolts" rather than "riots"? When does a revolt become a revolution?

During the week of April 23–30, 1968,
Students for a Democratic Society and
Students Afro-American Society rebelled
against the officials of Columbia University. One thousand police officers were
called in to clear the buildings and put
an end to violence. A second seizure of
Hamilton Hall ended in violent police
action on May 21–22. Education was
interrupted until the end of the academic year. Does the presence of police
on campuses contribute to the chaos?

4

Student Attitudes
and Concerns

by COX COMMISSION

General Characteristics

THE present generation of young people in our universities is the best informed, the most intelligent, and
the most idealistic this country has ever known. This
is the experience of teachers everywhere.

It is also the most sensitive to public issues and

From *Crisis at Columbia* by the Cox Commission (New York:
Vintage Books, 1968). pp. 4–6, 8–15. Copyright © 1968 by
Random House, Inc. Reprinted by permission of Random House,
Inc.

the most sophisticated in political tactics. Perhaps because they enjoy the affluence to support their ideals, today's undergraduate and graduate students exhibit, as a group, a higher level of social conscience than preceding generations.

The ability, social consciousness and conscience, political sensitivity, and honest realism of today's students are a prime cause of student disturbances. As one student observed during our investigation, today's students take seriously the ideals taught in schools and churches, and often at home, and then they see a system that denies its ideals in its actual life. Racial injustice and the war in Vietnam stand out as prime illustrations of our society's deviation from its professed ideals and of the slowness with which the system reforms itself. . . .

Many of these idealists have developed with considerable sophistication the thesis that these flaws are endemic* in the workings of American democracy. They argue that their form of pressure—direct action, confrontations, sit-ins, and (in some cases) physical violence—applied at points of institutional weakness, is a legitimate political tool comparable to the other forms of pressure—large political contributions, covert lobbying, favoritism, and the like—effectively applied by those who would lead society astray.

For some of these students their universities have become surrogates* for society. The university administration is close at hand. One can bedevil and strike out at it. If the frustrated activist cannot beat the system, he can at least insist that his own university should not lend itself to evil. There are a smaller

---

endemic—interwoven with.

surrogates—substitutes.

number who see the university as a place of shelter untouched by the evils of society. They suffer profound shock when they find that the university, and therefore they as parts of it, are not so far removed. In their view this makes them guilty of complicity in profound social and moral evil.

. . .

May not the fault lie with the older generation? Unless we are prepared to concede that ours is a sick society too corrupt to be saved, we must acknowledge that we have failed to transmit to many of the ablest young men and women either a sense of the values of reason, order, and civility or an appreciation of the fact that freedom depends upon voluntary restraint. We have managed to convey the idea that, because some of the values we upheld are outdated and others were always wrong, the remainder must also lack merit.

. . .

During the years in which the present university students were in secondary school the gap between the generations was widened by marked changes in speech, conduct, dress, and manners. Although older people generally disapproved the changes, the more exaggerated the new styles became the more they were promoted by entertainers and influential mass media. The cycle became self-sustaining. Inflated rhetoric and violence began to spread through contemporary society—again largely because the mass media give them the greatest attention. Among the young, inflated rhetoric and bizarre personal appearance have become symbolic behavior indicating disapproval of the "Establishment" and the older generation. . . .

The size and complexity of the large universities in an urban society increase the alienation of students and . . . there is too little at Columbia to offset the feeling. One form of response, which must be mentioned among the causes of violent demonstrations, is the romantic reaction against complexity, rationality, and restraint, which has become a small but pervasive thread in student life.

At Columbia more than a few students saw the barricading of the buildings in April as the moment when they began meaningful lives. They lived gloriously like revolutionary citizens of Paris. . . .

These general characteristics of student attitudes are intensified at Columbia by the urban environment and the conditions of student life. . . .

At Columbia, as at other universities, students' opinions cover the entire spectrum of political life. But two issues command unusually broad agreement among the young and engage their deepest emotions: the peace movement and racial justice. Both were causes of the April disturbances.

The War in Vietnam

During Dr. Truman's* testimony he observed:

Some of us have felt for a very long time that if it were inescapable that the current war in Vietnam had to continue on, it was debatable whether university communities could survive, because the tension is not only among students but in faculties, and the whole fabric of the institution is strained.

In a sense, I think there have been two battlefields in the war. One in Vietnam, and the other on our university campuses. And they are not good places for battlefields.

Dr. David Truman—vice-president of Columbia at the time of the riot and subsequent investigation.

One symbol of the student rebellion is this leader of the Students for a Democratic Society—the forefront of anti-Establishment protest. (UPI)

The Vietnam war is the overriding concern of nearly all students. For them it is a matter of life or death—to kill or be killed. For many, it is an immoral war and all who support it are immoral; it should be stopped at once—how stopped is a detail irrelevant to men of commitment. The consensus among students and most of the vocal intellectual community appears to validate their criticism, hence differing opinions are condemned with earnest righteousness.

The uncertainties of the draft, moreover, and the overbrooding threat of nuclear warfare have intensified every grievance and frustration.

Student opposition to the war has many forms. Student activists have taken part in nearly all the peace and anti-draft demonstrations. Just as some learned the tactics of obstructive protest in the civil rights movement others gained experience in rallies at draft boards and recruiting stations.*

.   .   .

In May 1965, violence broke out, which the City police were called to suppress, when protesters formed a human chain to block the Naval Reserve Officers Training Corps from entering Low Library† in order to hold final review ceremonies. On November 15, 1966, 200 students, organized by SDS, marched into Dodge Hall in order to "ask a few questions" of a recruiter for the Central Intelligence Agency (CIA) who was interviewing prospective applicants for employment. One day later, on November 16, 150 students marched to President Kirk's office in Low Library with a letter demanding an official statement of non-cooperation with the CIA. In February 1967, 18 students engaged in a sit-in demonstration, blocking access to the rooms in Dodge Hall where CIA interviews were to be conducted.

---

* We do not suggest that obstructive protest has been in any sense characteristic of either the civil rights or peace movements. Such tactics were exceptional and, at least in the civil rights movement, even those exceptions were usually associated with the unconstitutional suppression of other forms of expression.

† Low Library is the central administration building at Columbia. It is no longer used as a library.

On April 20, 1967, 300 SDS members and sympathizers filled the lobby of John Jay Hall where recruiters for the U.S. Marine Corps had set up tables. The next day 800 anti-recruiting demonstrators milled about Van Am Quadrangle, together with 500 counter-demonstrators sympathetic to campus recruiting. On February 28, 1968, a 200-man picket line, sponsored by SDS, marched toward Low Library in protest of the presence of recruiters for Dow Chemical Company; 80 Barnard and Columbia students left the march to stage a sit-in demonstration in Dodge Hall. On March 27, 1968, SDS led more than 100 students in a march through Low Library in a demonstration against the Institute for Defense Analyses.

We list these incidents here simply to show that issues connected with the Vietnam war had repeatedly stirred large demonstrations prior to last April's disturbances. . . .

Civil Rights and Community Relations

The cause of racial justice, more than any other issue, brought students out of the political lethargy of the 1950's and, like the Vietnam war, engrossed their deepest emotions. Today the "racism" they condemn encompasses not only active racial discrimination but continued acquiescence in the poverty, the denial of opportunity, and the human suffering that segregation in ghettos make integral parts of the Negro and Puerto Rican experience. Racial issues and the war on poverty also engage the active support of a larger segment of the student body than any other issue, with the possible exception of the war in Vietnam. At Columbia the presence of racial issues, symbolized by the projected gymnasium in Morning-

side Park, undoubtedly had much to do with the
breadth of the faculty and student support for those
who sparked the April uprising.

Columbia's location epitomizes the conflicts and
intensifies the emotional commitments and frustrations of the movement to relieve racism and poverty.
Situated on Morningside Heights, the University looks
down on the flats of Harlem, one of the most de-
pressed of all urban ghettos. Millions of black people
must have looked up at the institutional buildings as
symbols of the affluence of a white society; remote,
unattainable, and indifferent. Hundreds of Columbia
students who came to the University and then went
down into Harlem with high ideals of social justice,
but little prior experience with the realities of urban
poverty, have been shocked by immersion in the ghetto. Not only the strongest criticism of the projected
gymnasium but also important support for the seizure
of the buildings came from the College Citizenship
Council whose members were actively in touch with
Columbia's poorest neighbors.* A University official
suggested that the response of these students was a
case of well-intentioned but naive overreaction. Many
of us have also come to acquiesce in "the realities,"
with more or less discomfort, but one wonders whether the sensitive students' perception is not closer to
the truth.

Grievances and Problems of Black Students

One of the outstanding features of the most recent
wave of university demonstrations has been the cen-

---

* The Citizenship Council is engaged in important social service programs and other forms of community assistance in the
Morningside and Harlem areas. Many students contribute time
and energy to these activities and thus are drawn into continuous contact with the local areas.

Another symbol of student revolt is this black armed militant who occupied a building at Cornell. Black students are making increasing demands at colleges. (*The New York Times*)

tral role of self-conscious black students. Especially within the past year, Negro students on campuses, large and small, throughout the country have made unprecedented efforts to bring about changes in campus life increasing their participation and enhancing respect for their identity. Their goals included changes in curriculum, personnel, admissions, and living conditions. Sometimes they worked alone as more or less organized black students, sometimes in loose, temporary coalition with predominantly white organizations. Always they were moved by an intensely self-conscious design to act as black students and to make "black" a proud symbol. A recent accomplishment, mainly attributable to Negro college youth, is the unprecedented semantic reversal of the negative racial connotations formerly associated with the words "Negro" and especially "black."

Similarly, there is reason to think that the role of the black students at Columbia was uniquely important, for it may well have been their decision to request the white demonstrators to leave Hamilton Hall that converted a somewhat unfocused, noisy, disorderly, all-night demonstration into an unprecedented uprising involving the occupation of five campus buildings.

. . . Thus, black students have been profoundly influenced by, and react sharply to, shifts in the civil rights movement, just as they are extraordinarily sensitive to the political and cultural meanings and uses of race in contemporary society. The much publicized generation gap may well have even more effect upon black youths than others, for they are keenly aware that the movement for changes in the status of the Negro has been spearheaded by the young, especially by the initiative and energy of self-conscious, and increasingly race-conscious, Negroes in college. Public issues, such as the Vietnam war, the youth movement, and the worsening crisis of the ghettos, concern them no less than socially conscious white students, and probably not very differently except where their concern is racially self-conscious or influenced by a rather sophisticated awareness of the identity yet separateness of the demands being made by and for Negroes, the poor, and the young.

Thus, as students at Columbia, the black students are affected like all other students by their perceptions of the quality of student life and the apparent attitudes toward students of both faculty and Administration. Yet, even while they share this important degree of common experience with others, black students are uniquely influenced by their perception of the manner in which Columbia has dealt with small but successive generations of Negro students.

. . .

FURTHER INQUIRY

1. How do you account for the fact that the best informed student is often the most riotous?
2. To what extent may the cause of student riots lie with the older generation?
3. How do you account for the generation gap? Is it getting wider? How do you bridge the gap?
4. Do black students have special problems adjusting in a school like Columbia? Why or why not?
5. How are student disorders related to the war in Vietnam?

There are 275,000 high school students in New York City. The High School Student Union planned a boycott in May 1969 to enforce acceptance of the ten demands listed in the selection below. The boycott was largely ineffective. If you were a member of the Board of Education, how would you react to such demands?

5

High School Students of the City, Unite!

by FRED FERRETTI

"High school students are niggers. Depending upon how well you shuffle, you are paid, with grades and with recommendations for college."
—LAURIE SANDOW

"Outside agitators? The agitators are the students. Our principals and teachers don't seem to want to acknowledge that we can think. They should be proud of us. To say we're being led certainly doesn't

By Fred Ferretti in *New York*, April 28, 1969, vol. 2, no. 17, pp. 42–44. Copyright © 1969 by the New York Magazine Co. Reprinted by permission of the New York Magazine Co.

speak well for the school system. They're pointing out their own failure."

—CHARLOTTE BROWN

LAURIE SANDOW is 16 and white. Charlotte Brown is 18 and black. Both are students at the High School of Music and Art in upper Manhattan. Both are thoughtful, aware and earnest and believe that their public school education has been and is irrelevant. Both are part of a small group of high school students which less than a year ago devised and structured the High School Student Union and has nurtured it to the point where it now has the status—bestowed officially from the hip by the High School Principals' Association—of one of the "outside agitating forces" disrupting the city's high schools.

High school students like Laurie Sandow and Charlotte Brown admit that they agitate, but they contend that they and their union are constructive. The principals call their activities destructive. The High School Student Union agitates, its members maintain, because the high schools have trained students to fill preordained niches in a society they detest instead of educating them so that they can change that society. Agitation is necessary, the union contends, to dramatically call to the attention of educational and municipal authorities what it considers long-tolerated abuses in the high schools and the need for their reform. Says Charlotte Brown, "What's going on in the schools reflects what's going on outside. We want to be serene. We know long hair and pants aren't the thing. Students, in my opinion, are not out to slaughter teachers, not even out to give them a bad time. We're on their side, no matter what it looks like." . . .

The high school students' militancy takes many

The Weakly Reader, published by high school students in New York. The cover cartoon shows students bowing before a teacher who is explaining how fortunate they are to have a faculty that will work overtime to make up "pay—uh, I mean education" lost during the school strikes. (*The New York Times*)

forms. On its simplest level it can be long hair, off-beat clothing, outrageous, attention-getting behavior and perhaps vandalism. Underground high school newspapers have sprung up, most of them styled after *Rat, The East Village Other, The New York Free Press,* and *Screw.* The students use such names for their papers as *The Daily Planet, Institutional Green,* and *The New York Herald Tribune.* There also exists HIPS, the High School Independent Press Service, which supplies the many papers. The parent newspaper, the official organ of the union, is the *High School Free Press:* "Of, by and for liberated high school students."

The papers devote articles to such subjects as the recent peace march to Central Park; revolution at the Dalton School; the Army mutiny at the Presidio; legalization of marijuana; New York City politics and Board of Education policies. . . .

The *Free Press* is more or less run by Howard Swerdloff, also a member of the small group of students who founded the union. The circulation claimed by the *Free Press* ranges from 10,000 to 50,000.

. . . The Student Union is currently in the midst of what it calls its Spring Offensive. A list of 10 demands upon the Board of Education has been drawn up, has been published in the *Free Press,* and was formally presented this month. A boycott by as many as possible of the 275,000 students in the city's 90 high schools is planned early in May, perhaps May 1, to enforce the demands.

Says Laurie Sandow: "The high schools have been blowing up. That's one thing. Spring is that kind of season, isn't it? But our demands are something else. They will culminate in a walkout around the beginning of May."

How long will it last?

"If we go out, we'll stay out. And we hope every-body who goes out will stay out. We're afraid that some kids will stay out for a while, then go back because they'll be told they're missing their education. If they go back for that they'll be totally missing our point."

It is only recently that the High School Student Union has acquired muscle. It still is an amorphous organization, without any officers, but with a Repre-sentative Committee and an office staff and locals in most of the city's high schools. . . .

The Student Union had its beginnings just before the summer of 1968. Prior to that, an organization existed calling itself the High School Students' Mobili-zation Committee to End the War in Vietnam. It shared offices with the Fifth Avenue Vietnam Peace Parade Committee. Its function was to act as the student arm of the peace movement. Its members ran off and distributed leaflets and generally helped in the day-to-day drudgery of the Fifth Avenue Com-mittee's organizing efforts. The students were gener-ally peace-oriented. They included some incubating members of Students for a Democratic Society as well as "lots of kids who were red diaper babies, whose parents were former Communists, or who were in the Movement," says Charlotte. The SDS-oriented students were, she said, "basically anti-Communist because they felt the Communist Party was too con-servative for them."

.   .   .

It would appear that the union, being leaderless, would also be headless. "High school students real-ize," says Laurie, "that when you have a leader, you look to that leader. You look to see how he goes. When he's not there you don't know which way to go. We don't want to have to depend on one person, so we have no leaders." The union's general rule appears to be that everybody contributes what he does best for the general betterment of the Student Union.

What makes someone declare for and become committed to an organization like the Student Union?

"When I was in tenth grade at Music and Art, I had no history," said Laurie, who made her first peace march in 1966, when she was 13. "In eleventh grade I got history. History is hypocritical knowledge. You study the Constitution; it says all Americans have equal rights, but the black man is classified as three-fifths of a man. You read that our country is founded on laws and we go to war in Vietnam in violation of our Constitution. We violate the laws of the United Nations. We violate the Geneva agreements we agreed to abide by.

"The country is founded on racism, whether it likes to admit it or not. In very subtle ways, throughout your school life, racist values are inculcated, as are values which preserve the status quo. When people talk about the beginnings of this country they say it all began with Columbus. Maybe they say they recognize that the Indians were here when he came.

"You study the settlement of the West. There's a euphemism, the settlement of the West. You find that when the settlement of the West began there were one million Indians. When it was finished there were 500,000 Indians. The phrase *manifest destiny* is used as justification for our expansion and slaughter. It's amazing that this racism was *just* discovered with the Kerner report, isn't it?"

Says Charlotte: "I grew up in a ghetto. I reacted against my own parents, against my neighborhood. I saw people trapped in their own poverty. Now I'm in a 'good' school so I'm supposed to be a little bet-

"I was for peace . . . but the only time anybody listens

(UPI)

to you in this society, it seems, is when there is violence."

ter off. It's not true. You know, I would have liked to have had an unhassled childhood.

"I was for peace. You take these SDS kids. Most of them were Peace Corps. They wanted civil rights. They used to be pacifists. Because of the responses they got they became more radical. The only time anybody listens to you in this society, it seems, is when there is violence. We, I, am infected with this society's values.

"School teaches you to live in society as it now exists. It teaches you to follow, not to lead. Certain people, mainly black, are reserved for the Army, for factories, to be secretaries or maids."

Says Laurie, "When you're in elementary school you go home for lunch. Not in high school. They're afraid you're going to get into trouble. They're supposed to be delegating responsibility as you get older. You know what they're worried about? That you won't come back to school once you get out.

"You know society says, 'We need workers.' Wouldn't it be catastrophic if *all* the kids wanted, *wanted,* to paint, to write music or poetry? Who would be around to fill the jobs? There is an existing caste system and class system that has to be preserved or the whole thing will fall apart."

.   .   .

In its early days the structure of the Student Union was even more formless than it is now. "People just got together to talk to each other," Charlotte says. "We had only a vague desire to heighten the radical consciousness of the student. We talked, of course. And what yelling! And the male chauvinism! Wow! It's there. It's all there. And the personality conflicts! But what gradually came out, the most important thing, was that although it was important for us to seek to change the Establishment, it was more important for us to change our own heads.

"We're restructuring ourselves now. We were white-middle-class-oriented. Now we're going to talk with the black student organizations." Laurie agrees that white students must begin to think black, "to work with the Black Student Union, while knowing that we really can't join together because now two different frames of reference are involved." Some sort of amalgamation of the High School Student Union, the Black Student Union and the African-American Students' Association will probably come to pass this spring. A force could thus be created that the school authorities might have to deal with on an at least quasi-formal basis.

There is evidence that the Board of Education is listening to the Union. A couple of weeks ago a representative of the Board called the *Free Press* to ask if the list of 10 demands could be read to him over the phone.

He was told to buy the paper.

What They Want

The following are the High School Student Union's 10 demands, the price asked to prevent a Student Union-sponsored boycott of the high schools this May. There is virtually no chance that they will be considered with any seriousness by the Board of Education.

1. No more suspensions, involuntary transfers, discharges, detention, no harassment of students.

2. No cops in schools.

3. No program cards; no hall checks, lunchroom checks or bathroom passes.

4. An end to General and Commercial diplomas.

General diplomas are "tickets to the Army." Commercial diplomas imply training for jobs "that don't exist any more." A high school diploma for all.

5. Open admission to all colleges, including private colleges within the city.

6. Jobs and housing be made available to every student whether he is a dropout or a graduate.

7. No military recruitment in the schools.

8. Black studies and Latin studies departments controlled by the students, as a way of eliminating racism.

9. Community control of the schools.

10. Power. We want student power.

FURTHER INQUIRY

1. Should a school teach a student to adjust to society or to change it? Justify your point of view.

2. To what extent are the demands of the high school students achievable?

3. What is your opinion on student power? How can it be achieved? How can it be used constructively?

4. Do you agree or disagree with Laurie's criticism of America's history? Justify your position.

5. Laurie said, "white students must begin to think black." Do you agree? Why or why not?

6. Of the ten student demands, which, if any, have been achieved?

The description given here is from an account written more than 100 years ago. Nat Turner was one of a very few slaves who learned to read and write. He led a slave army armed with hoes, axes, scythes, and shovels in an unsuccessful rebellion in Virginia. What connection, if any, is there between education and riots?

6

Nat Turner's Insurrection

by THOMAS WENTWORTH HIGGINSON

. . . IN the woods on the plantation of Joseph Travis [August 21, 1831], six slaves met at noon for what is called in the Northern States a picnic and in the Southern a barbecue. . . . In this plot four of the men had been already initiated,—Henry, Hark or Hercules, Nelson, and Sam. Two others were novices, Will and Jack by name. The party had re-

Excerpts from Thomas Wentworth Higginson, "Nat Turner's Insurrection," *Atlantic Monthly*, VIII (August, 1861), pp. 173–87.

mained together from twelve to three o'clock, when a seventh man joined them,—a short, stout, powerfully built person, of dark mulatto complexion and strongly-marked African features, but with a face full of expression and resolution. This was Nat Turner.

He was at this time nearly thirty-one years old, having been born on the second of October, 1800. He had belonged originally to Benjamin Turner—whence his last name, slaves having usually no patronymic,*—had been transferred to Putnam Moore, and then to his present owner. He had, by his own account, felt himself singled out from childhood for some great work; and he had some peculiar marks on his person, which, joined to his great mental precocity, were enough to occasion, among his youthful companions, a superstitious faith in his gifts and destiny. He had great mechanical ingenuity also, experimentalized very early in making paper, gunpowder, pottery, and in other arts which in later life he was found thoroughly to understand. His moral faculties were very strong, so that white witnesses admitted that he had never been known to swear an oath, to drink a drop of spirits, or to commit a theft. And in general, so marked were his early peculiarities, that people said "he had too much sense to be raised, and if he was, he would never be of any use as a slave." This impression of personal destiny grew with his growth;—he fasted, prayed, preached, read the Bible, heard voices when he walked behind his plough, and communicated his revelations to the awe-struck slaves. They told him in return that, "if they had his sense, they would not serve any master in the world." ...

_____

patronymic—name derived from the father.

Whatever Nat Turner's experiences of slavery might have been, it is certain that his plans were not suddenly adopted, but that he had brooded over them for years. . . .

When he came, therefore, to the barbecue on the appointed Sunday, and found not these four only, but two others, his first question to the intruders was, How they came thither. To this Will answered manfully, that his life was worth no more than the others, and "his liberty was as dear to him." This admitted him to confidence, and as Jack was known to be entirely under Hark's influence, the strangers were no bar to their discussion. . . .

John Brown* invaded Virginia with nineteen men, and with the avowed resolution to take no life but in self-defence. Nat Turner attacked Virginia from within, with six men, and with the determination to spare no life until his power was established. John Brown intended to pass rapidly through Virginia, and then retreat to the mountains. Nat Turner intended to "conquer Southampton County as the white men did in the Revolution, and then retreat, if necessary, to the Dismal Swamp." . . .

We must pass over the details of horror, as they occurred during the next twenty-four hours. Swift and stealthy as Indians, the black men passed from house to house,—not pausing, not hesitating, as their terrible work went on. In one thing they were humaner than Indians or than white men fighting against Indians,—there was no gratuitous outrage beyond the death-blow itself, no insult, no mutilation; but in every house they entered, that blow fell on man, woman, and child,—nothing that had a white skin

_____

John Brown—abolitionist who resorted to violence in an effort to end slavery.

was spared. From every house they took arms and ammunition, and from a few, money; on every plantation they found recruits: those dusky slaves, so obsequious to their masters the day before, so prompt to sing and dance before his Northern visitors, were all swift to transform themselves into fiends of retribution now; show them sword or musket and they grasped it, though it were an heirloom from Washington himself. The troop increased from house to house,—first to fifteen, then to forty, then to sixty. Some were armed with muskets, some with axes, some with scythes; some came on their masters' horses. As the numbers increased, they could be divided, and the awful work was carried on more rapidly still. The plan then was for an advanced guard of horsemen to approach each house at a gallop, and surround it till the others came up. Meanwhile what agonies of terror must have taken place within, shared alike by innocent and guilty! what memories of wrongs inflicted on those dusky creatures, by some,—what innocent participation, by others, in the penance! The outbreak lasted for but forty-eight hours; but during that period fifty-five whites were slain, without the loss of a single slave.

One fear was needless, which to many a husband and father must have intensified the last struggle. These negroes had been systematically brutalized from childhood; they had been allowed no legalized or permanent marriage; they had beheld around them an habitual licentiousness* such as can scarcely exist except in a Slave State; some of them had seen their wives and sisters habitually polluted by the husbands and the brothers of these fair white women who were now absolutely in their power. Yet I have looked

---

licentiousness—disregard for social and moral rules.

through the Virginia newspapers of that time in vain for one charge of an indecent outrage on a woman against these triumphant and terrible slaves. Wherever they went, there went death, and that was all. Compare this with ordinary wars; compare it with the annals of the French Revolution. . . .

When the number of adherents had increased to fifty or sixty, Nat Turner judged it time to strike at the county-seat, Jerusalem. . . . On the way it was necessary to pass the plantation of Mr. Parker, three miles from Jerusalem. Some of the men wished to stop here and enlist some of their friends. Nat Turner objected, as the delay might prove dangerous; he yielded at last, and it proved fatal.

He remained at the gate with six or eight men; thirty or forty went to the house, half a mile distant. They remained too long, and he went alone to hasten them. During his absence a party of eighteen white men came up suddenly, dispersing the small guard left at the gate; and when the main body of slaves emerged from the house, they encountered, for the first time, their armed masters. . . .

Sadly came Nat Turner at nightfall into those gloomy woods where forty-eight hours before he had revealed the details of his terrible plot to his companions. At the outset all his plans had succeeded; everything was as he predicted: the slaves had come readily at his call, the masters had proved perfectly defenseless. Had he not been persuaded to pause at Parker's plantation, he would have been master before now of the arms and ammunition at Jerusalem; and with these to aid, and the Dismal Swamp for a refuge, he might have sustained himself indefinitely against his pursuers.

Now the blood was shed, the risk was incurred,

The discovery of Nat Turner during that first "long hot summer." (Kean Archives)

his friends were killed or captured, and all for what? . . .

On Sunday, October 30th, a man named Benjamin Phipps, going out for the first time on patrol duty, was passing at noon a clearing in the woods where a number of pine-trees had long since been felled. There was a motion among their boughs; he stopped to watch it; and through a gap in the branches he saw, emerging from a hole in the earth beneath, the face of Nat Turner. Aiming his gun instantly, Phipps called on him to surrender. The fugitive, exhausted with watching and privation, entangled in the branches, armed only with a sword, had nothing to do but to yield; . . . [After two months of hiding] his insurrection ended where it began; for this spot was only a mile and a half from the house of Joseph Travis. . . .

When Nat Turner was asked by Mr. T. R. Gray, the counsel assigned him, whether, although defeated, he still believed in his own Providential mission, he answered, as simply as one who came thirty years after him, "Was not Christ crucified?" In the same spirit, when arraigned before the court, "he answered, 'Not guilty,' saying to his counsel that he did not feel so." But apparently no argument was made in his favor by his counsel, nor were any witnesses called,—he being convicted on the testimony of Levi Waller, and upon his own confession, which was put in by Mr. Gray, and acknowledged by the prisoner before the six justices composing the court, as being "full, free, and voluntary." He was therefore placed in the paradoxical position of conviction by his own confession, under a plea of "Not guilty." The arrest took place on the thirtieth of October, 1831, the confession on the first of November, the trial and conviction on the fifth, and the execution on the following Friday, the eleventh of November. . . .

FURTHER INQUIRY

1. To what extent do the feelings of Nat Turner resemble those of black militant leaders today?
2. Why did Nat Turner feel that the Bible justified his rebellion?
3. Is the Nat Turner uprising properly included in a book on riots? Why or why not?
4. Why is the rebellion only briefly mentioned in most textbooks?
5. How do you account for the fact that at his trial Nat Turner declared that he was "not guilty"?
6. What effect did Nat Turner's rebellion have upon the South? the North?

Major riots in the history of the United
States whose causes remind us of present-
day conditions were the New York City
draft riots of July 13–16, 1863. These
riots were in reaction to the Civil War
which was considered "a rich·man's war,
a poor man's fight." To what extent have
our present attitudes about conscription*
changed?

7

The Bloody Week

by WILLARD A. HEAPS

THE United States was in the throes of a tragic division in 1863. When the Southern states seceded from
the Union in the spring of 1861, the Northerners
had felt certain that their industrial superiority would
make the war short. But the Confederacy proved to
be a stubborn, dedicated, and unyielding foe. At the

---

conscription—compulsory enrollment of men for service
in the armed forces.

From *Riots, U.S.A. 1765–1965* by Willard A. Heaps (New
York: The Seabury Press, 1966), pp. 50–60. Copyright © by
Willard A. Heaps. Reprinted by permission of The Seabury
Press, New York.

beginning of 1863 the Union Army needed more men than the volunteer system could supply.

After heated discussion the United States Congress passed the National Conscription Act, which was signed by President Lincoln on March 3. This legislation was the first in which the Federal government sought to create a citizen army without the aid of state authorities, and the first to fix the principle that every able-bodied male citizen had an obligation to perform military service. Men between the ages of twenty and forty-five were to be enrolled, and if their names were drawn they would serve for three years.

An objectionable and troublemaking feature of the Act was the provision that anyone whose name was drawn could pay three hundred dollars to the local draft board for a substitute or furnish his own acceptable replacement. This obviously favored the rich, for the weekly wage of the average laborer was twenty dollars.

The Act had established a quota of 300,000; New York City's was 33,000. The enrollment, in a house-to-house canvass, was completed on June 29, and the drawings were set to begin on Saturday, July 11, 1863. This interval unfortunately permitted the development of vigorous opposition among the poor of the city, particularly the Irish, who formed a quarter of the 800,000 population. About 10 per cent of the city's foreign-born were known criminals. The poor thoroughly resented the exemption clause, voicing their disapproval with the cry, "A rich man's war, a poor man's fight!"

New York City had been divided into congressional districts, six in Manhattan, each under the supervision of a provost marshal, with a civilian draft board and a doctor. The eligibles were not given draft cards, as in the World War I draft and subsequent years. Their names, written on slips of paper, were placed in a revolving wooden box or lottery wheel, from which the quota number would be drawn by a civilian.

The initial drawing in the Ninth District office at Third Avenue and Forty-sixth Street took place on Saturday, the eleventh, and seven hundred names were read off without incident. But opponents—war-weary Democrats, Southern sympathizers, and Confederate agitators—were active on Sunday. By Monday morning they had set the stage for what were to become the longest, most widespread, and most destructive riots in American history, with by far the largest number of rioters.

The four-day New York City Draft Riots were unique in several features. The participants totaled seventy thousand, swarming through the streets at times in screaming, frenzied herds of ten thousand. Since the police force amounted to a little over two thousand, they were often outnumbered by five hundred to one. The riotous mobs did not limit their ravages to a single neighborhood or area, as is usual in riots, but instead covered all parts of the city from downtown Manhattan to Harlem, and on both the east and west sides of the Fifth Avenue dividing line in what is now midtown.

Nor were the riots confined to a single day, or even the daylight hours; four days and nights, even until the early morning, the crowds roamed the city without pause in a continuous orgy of destruction. They committed every sort of crime—murder, lynching, looting, and burning. One of the city's newspapers correctly called the riots "a carnival of violence."

The riots started as a treasonable insurrection against the United States Government, then became a destructive attack against the well-to-do, and finally a race riot with Negroes as targets. Scores of separate incidents were equal in fury to many full-scale riots.

The New York City Draft Riots offer the best single example of a mob expanding its original objective to anarchy and every sort of crime and violence.

Seldom has a mob taken over a metropolis and terrified its citizens so completely before being subdued by artillery and musket fire. The range of mob activities was so vast and the countless individual outbursts of such savage fury and appalling destruction that only a few of the highlights can be mentioned.

.   .   .

At the appointed hour of 10 A.M.* the front doors of the draft office were opened and those nearest the door poured in. The regular turns of the wheel had produced about a hundred names, each called out, when suddenly a large paving block came crashing through the window, followed immediately by a pistol shot and a shower of stones and bricks.

The time was ten thirty-five. The riot had begun.

The mob rushed the door, overwhelming the police guard. The draft wheel was destroyed and all the records were torn to bits. Someone spread turpentine on the floor and set the office ablaze. Soon dense smoke began to pour into the street, and some of the cheering crowd beat the firemen off when they attempted to attach the hoses to the hydrants. Within an hour the entire block from Forty-sixth to Forty-seventh streets was in flames.

John Kennedy, the superintendent of police, approached the spot in civilian clothes but was recognized and beaten into insensibility before being

_____
Monday, July 13, 1863.

Opposition to the draft did not start with the youth of today. In 1863 a mob violently opposed to the draft burned and ransacked houses in New York (facing page), burned the provost marshal's office (above), and fought with the militia (below). (Kean Archives)

The 1863 anti-draft riots were caused by ethnic problems as well as strong objection to the National Conscription Act. In this picture a Negro is hung and burned during that riot. (Kean Archives)

rescued. Meanwhile arriving police detachments, outnumbered two hundred to one, were overwhelmed by the savage mob and escaped only by a miracle. A unit of locally stationed Federal soldiers armed with sabers and muskets was met by a shower of paving stones and brickbats. . . .

. . .

Led by a giant thug waving a sledge hammer, a group attempted to force the entrance door and managed to smash in a panel. The first to crawl through was killed instantly. The sight of his headless and bloody body served to renew the mob's rage. They came on again with sledges and crowbars, and formed human battering rams with telephone poles. The police inside escaped through a rear smoke exhaust pipe.

When the doors gave way the rioters swarmed on the various floors, a few making their way to the top-floor drill room to seize the precious carbines and ammunition stored there. They barricaded the door so that they would not be discovered. From every window of the factory carbines were thrown to those waiting below. Others formed a human chain along which the guns were passed out to the street.

Police officers using their clubs freely were finally able to clear a path to the doorway. Fearing that those inside would be arrested, some rioters set fire to the building in a dozen places. The flames spread rapidly, and those on the first floor were clubbed unmercifully by the waiting police as they tried to escape. The looters on the fifth floor found themselves trapped by the flames when they opened the barricaded door. Some leaped to their deaths from the windows. Many more were killed in the roaring inferno when the floor collapsed at about 4:30 P.M. The dead were never counted, for only bones and ashes were later found. In the entire four-hour attack, twenty-five rioters were known to have been killed and more than seventy-five seriously wounded. Two thousand finished carbines had been stolen and were to be put to good use.

. . .

Another group had meanwhile attacked the draft office of the Eighth District at Broadway and Twenty-eighth Street and both looted and burned the entire block in which it was located. . . .

The race riot within this many-faceted riot began in the afternoon. Negroes on the street were attacked and beaten soundly, on the pretext that they were responsible for the war, hence the draft. While the *Tribune* was being assaulted a large mob visited a nearby Negro section, throwing furniture into the street and burning it and, finally, an entire block of rickety houses. Every colored person attempting to escape was punished by a beating.

The first Negro lynching occurred early on Monday evening. Several hundred men and boys seized a helpless colored man, beat him into insensibility, hanged him by a rope thrown over the limb of a tree, hacked his body, and finally built a fire to roast the corpse. A few hours later a Negro mother was beaten to death while attempting to protect her crippled son.

.   .   .

By Tuesday morning state militiamen were being mobilized and the mayor had asked that Federal troops be sent to the city from Gettysburg. . . .

.   .   .

The day began with the early morning murders of two Negroes. The houses of the colored people throughout the city were almost systematically plundered and burned and three more victims were murdered after dark.

.   .   .

Roving gangs covered every section of the city while the major outbreaks were taking place. The day was one of great robberies. Hundreds of stores, including the famous Brooks Brothers, were looted. The deserted homes of the wealthy were plundered and, in some cases, burned.

.   .   .

Tuesday had proved to be the height of the

violence, but the uprising was far from finished. Governor Seymour of New York belatedly issued a proclamation declaring the city to be in a state of insurrection. But five regiments of troops were en route, and the reign of the rabble would inevitably be finished.

The orgy of murder and pillage continued on Wednesday. Three more Negroes were lynched, many were beaten and their tenement homes sacked and burned. A reporter characterized the chase thus: "It was a case of the hares and the hounds."

.   .   .

Fresh Federal troops poured into the beleaguered city on Thursday, and the constant patrols prevented the formation of mobs. The few last-ditch pockets of resistance were successfully broken up. The riots were over.

The weary police and soldiers began attempting to recover the stolen loot. Damage claims amounting to two million dollars (the present-day equivalent of ten million) were paid from a Riot Damage Indemnity Fund raised by bond issues. Business loss was incalculable.

The most quoted figure of killed was one thousand, but a maximum of five hundred seems more nearly accurate. The number of seriously wounded was reliably stated at nearly a thousand. More than four hundred police and three hundred militiamen and soldiers suffered serious injury. . . .

The government never even considered abolishing the draft in New York City, and the clause permitting payment for a substitute remained in effect. The enrollment records of the two burned district offices had been saved, and the drawings resumed on August 25 under the protection of Federal soldiers who had remained in the city.

The July terror in New York City has been termed by one of its historians "the largest violent, most brutal outbreak in our country's history."

FURTHER INQUIRY

1. If the Federal Government had enlisted aid from state authorities before passing the conscription act, do you think the riot would have occurred? Why or why not?
2. Why was it unfair to exempt from the draft those citizens who could pay three hundred dollars?
3. Why do you think the rioters felt that Negroes were responsible for the war?
4. What similarities and differences do you see between the anti-draft riots of 1863 and the anti-draft riots of today?

In 1892, the workers at the Carnegie
Steel Company plant in Homestead,
Pennsylvania, went on strike. In those
days the strike was not yet considered
an appropriate part of collective bar-
gaining between labor and capital.
Before the strike ended bloody rioting
took place. The strikes of the past often
led to riots. Today's strikes are usually
peaceful. How do you explain the
change?

8

Steel Lockout: The Bloodiest Capital-Labor Conflict

by WILLARD A. HEAPS

As IN all riots, a particular incident or situation triggers the mob violence. In labor conflicts this is most
often the hiring of nonunion workmen (scabs) in
place of the strikers. Resentment of the strikebreakers, often imported from outside the immediate strike
area, stiffens the resistance and obstinacy of the

From *Riots, U.S.A. 1765–1965* by Willard A. Heaps (New
York: The Seabury Press, 1966), pp. 73–84. Copyright © by
Willard A. Heaps. Reprinted by permission of The Seabury
Press, New York.

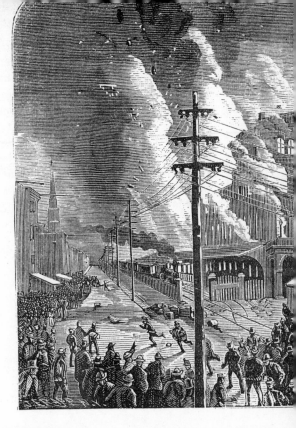

To gain recognition of unions, American workingmen in the 1870s engaged in violent acts. One such act is the

strikers and may incite them to extreme and unrestrained acts. Sometimes an unyielding resistance on the part of the employers manifested by a threatening or challenging statement or an ill-timed act will lead to lawlessness.

In the 1892 strike of workers at the Carnegie Steel Company in Homestead, Pennsylvania, the violence, unparalleled in a labor-management dispute before or since, followed a long-planned lockout which was to have been enforced by a substantial

burning of the Union Depot in Pittsburgh during the railroad strike in 1877. (Kean Archives)

number of hired and imported private police. The strikers reacted with savage violence against those brought into the community to protect strikebreakers. The Homestead lockout has been appropriately characterized as "one of the great battles for workers' rights" and "a battle which for bloodthirstiness and boldness could not be excelled in actual warfare."

.   .   .

The mill, fronting the curving waterfront for a mile, dominated the town. Operating around the

119

clock, its chimneys continually belched out acrid and poisonous smoke, dust, dirt, and cinders (this was long before the subject of air pollution was even dreamed of), so that sunlight was seldom able to penetrate the ever present dark pall. At night the sky was lit by the blazing fires of the furnaces. The river water was contaminated by industrial wastes and sewage from upstream. Homestead was a desolate, dirty, and depressing town.

Conditions for the majority of the workers were deplorable. The unskilled day laborers (primarily Slavs, called dinkey men or bohunks) were paid fourteen cents an hour—$9.80 a week, the equivalent of less than $40 today. However, the earnings of skilled laborers, the aristocrats of the work force, were excellent—as much as $70 a week ($280 by today's standards). But all steelworkers more than earned their wages. Working conditions were appalling: twelve-hour shifts, seven-day weeks, temperatures of 130 degrees, no time out for meals, no washing-up facilities, and no compensation for injuries. The year before the strike three hundred men were killed and two thousand injured on the job in the mills around Pittsburgh alone.

. . . Andrew Carnegie, the firm's head, was publicly on record as favoring unions and approving them as a part of the ideal employer-employee relationship. Privately he opposed them.

The company's chairman and general manager, Henry Clay Frick, . . . was an outspoken anti-unionist; he had repeatedly stated that unions should not exist. . . .

Six months after he joined Carnegie in 1889, Frick had settled a strike at Homestead only by making concessions. His opposition to the Amalgamated union was therefore strengthened. The showdown came as soon as the three-year union-management contract approached its expiration date of June 30, 1892.

. . .

The union members called for a strike on July 2 and were joined by the three thousand nonunion mechanics and common laborers. The battle lines were drawn. Frick had decided to break the union at Homestead. Even before the deadline date he had begun signing up skilled workers from other companies and, as his trump card, had recruited a force of three hundred armed Pinkerton detectives to protect the works and the imported scabs. These paid guards, from Chicago and New York, were to gather at Ashtabula, Ohio, on Lake Erie, a mid-point between the two cities, on the morning of July 5 and proceed by rail to Youngstown. From there they were to be transported at night by boat up the Monongahela River to Homestead. Since it might prove illegal to bring an armed force into the state of Pennsylvania, the rifles, pistols, billy clubs, and ammunition were to be shipped separately. The guards were to be armed after they were within the state boundaries.

. . .

When the contract deadline was not met, Frick began to shut down the works. By the thirtieth of June the entire work force was locked out. To strengthen the security of the plant, a fence fifteen feet high was built around it, extending to the river's edge. This was of solid boards topped with barbed wire and with holes spaced along its three-mile length, presumably for armed guards.

Though Frick had asked for a force of county deputies to protect the plant, none could apparently be recruited, so the Pinkerton men were to be deputized once they had landed on the company property.

By July 5 the force of 316 Pinkertons had assembled at the designated spot below Homestead. In addition to the professionals, the motley crowd of "detectives" included toughs, criminals, jobless drifters, and college students on vacation. They were told only that they had been hired by a corporation as guards. They were armed with two hundred and fifty Winchester rifles, three hundred pistols, and ammunition. Like an army unit, they were dressed in uniforms of slouch hats with colorful bands and dark blue trousers with lighter stripes.

The strikers never for a moment underestimated the tactics Frick might employ, and so they established an elaborate system of scouts and guards to keep abreast of developments.

The expedition set out shortly after midnight on July 6, 1892, the two barges at first being towed by two tugs—then, after an engine failure, by one. Each Pinkerton man was armed and given fifty rounds of ammunition during the four-hour trip. But such a movement could scarcely remain secret, and a union lookout at Pittsburgh telegraphed Homestead: "Watch the river. Steamer with barges left here."

When the tug was approaching the spot selected for the landing inside the plant grounds, the pilot sounded the required steam whistle to indicate a landing. This was the signal for the town to come alive. Strikers joined citizens in rushing to the banks of the Monongahela River. Hundreds of armed strikers running along the shore fired into the pitch-blackness of the river. The approach to the river side of the plant, however, was blocked by the fence. In a single moment the crowd knocked over the obstruction and rushed pell-mell to the spot where the two barges were pulled up parallel to the shore line. At this time the protesters were estimated to number close to ten thousand men, women and boys, all bearing weapons—pistols, revolvers, rifles, clubs, sticks, or stones. At the landing all was strangely silent; each side appeared to be awaiting a first move by the other.

The leader of the Pinkerton forces shouted a warning that his men were coming ashore, he had hoped peacefully, to occupy the works. When the gangplank had been laid, several strikers attempted to dislodge it without success. Jeers and stones greeted the first rifle-carrying blue-clad enemy on the plank. But as more stepped forward (forty had volunteered) a hail of bullets killed one and seriously wounded five. Other Pinkertons returned the fire and their bullets found ready marks in the dense crowd. More than thirty fell wounded and two were killed instantly. The firing by both sides continued even after the guards sought shelter below deck. This first encounter had lasted only three minutes.

During the lull the strikers erected steel and wooden barriers at the top of the steep bank, the wounded and dead were removed, and the noncombatants and women moved away from the line of fire, to observe better the inevitable continuation of the battle. The Pinkerton tug meanwhile left for Pittsburgh with the wounded under a barrage of gunfire.

Daylight was approaching and the stalemate must be broken. A representative of the strikers attempted to obtain the surrender of the hirelings, but the answer, shouted to all within range, was "If you don't withdraw, we will mow every one of you down." At eight o'clock a second landing attempt resulted in more killed and wounded on both sides, and spasmodic firing continued for more than two more hours. But the Pinkerton men, sheltered below the decks of the barges, could only fire through the limited number of portholes, with little range.

Now the strikers and their sympathizers had gained the advantage, and they sought to flush out their trapped quarry on the barges. Dynamite sticks proved effective only when thrown from nearby boats; even then the damage was slight. Civil War cannons were then fired from both sides of the river, but they, too, were relatively ineffective.

Then the strikers remembered the plant's oil stored in tanks. Pumping the oil into the river upstream from the barges, they attempted to start a fire without success. Next they ignited a raft loaded with greasy cloths and oil and cast it adrift, but the current floated the raft safely past the barges. Finally a small car loaded with blazing barrels of oil was rolled down the expanse of the bank but was deflected from its course before reaching the waterline. Sporadic gunfire continued during all these attempts at barge burning.

When the tug returned from Pittsburgh and tried to approach the barges to pull them free from the shore, the fire from the hundreds of armed strikers was so intense that it quickly retreated.

The impasse continued. The Pinkerton forces had several times waved white surrender handkerchiefs through portholes, only to have them shot away. For three afternoon hours the union and strike leaders attempted to reason with the mob, to convince them that further violence would inevitably lead to more casualties, and that nothing could possibly be gained by a continuation of the fighting. The more determined and excited strikers resisted these appeals. But the arguments of reason finally prevailed, and at about five o'clock the surrender negotiations were completed.

The casualties of this "shocking, sickening, unciv-ilized day" were never accurately totaled. The most reliable figure was at least thirty-five strikers and Pinkertons dead and four hundred injured, many of them seriously.

The Homestead strike was not a spontaneous up-rising on the part of unorganized workers. It was a war between one of the most powerful of the great modern corporations (the expanding Carnegie Steel Company became the United States Steel Corpora-tion) and what was then one of the strongest unions in the country.

The company won and the riotous strikers lost in what was one of the more tragic chapters in the history of United States labor-management relations.

FURTHER INQUIRY

1. Do you believe in the right of unions to strike? All unions? When do you feel that a union does not have the right to strike?
2. Why were Frick and the Carnegie Steel Company so antiunion?
3. The company "lost the battle but won the war." Why was this so? What were the great weapons that business could use against labor unions?
4. Why are striking unions so much more suc-cessful today?
5. Is a strike a riot? Why or why not?

For months there was resentment by servicemen, civilians, and police toward those who wore drape coats and dangling watch chains—the zoot-suiters. A riot erupted following the beating of a couple of servicemen by a gang of zoot-suiters in Los Angeles in June 1943. It was believed that the honor of one uniform against the other was at stake. Similar actions took place in San Diego, Philadelphia, Chicago, and Detroit. How did these incidents reflect the nature of American ethnic and race relations in the 1940s?

9

The Zoot-Suit Riot

by CAREY MCWILLIAMS

ON Monday evening, June seventh, thousands of *Angelenos,* in response to twelve hours' advance notice in the press, turned out for a mass lynching. Marching through the streets of downtown Los An-

From *North from Mexico,* by Carey McWilliams, pp. 248–51. Copyright 1948 by Carey McWilliams. Reprinted by permission of the author.

geles, a mob of several thousand soldiers, sailors, and civilians, proceeded to beat up every zoot-suiter they could find. Pushing its way into the important motion picture theaters, the mob ordered the management to turn on the house lights and then ranged up and down the aisles dragging Mexicans out of their seats. Street cars were halted while Mexicans, and some Filipinos and Negroes, were jerked out of their seats, pushed into the streets, and beaten with sadistic frenzy. If the victims wore zoot-suits, they were stripped of their clothing and left naked or half-naked on the streets, bleeding and bruised. Proceeding down Main Street from First to Twelfth, the mob stopped on the edge of the Negro district. Learning that the Negroes planned a warm reception for them, the mobsters turned back and marched through the Mexican east side spreading panic and terror. . . .

Throughout the night the Mexican communities were in the wildest possible turmoil. Scores of Mexican mothers were trying to locate their youngsters and several hundred Mexicans milled around each of the police substations and the Central Jail trying to get word of missing members of their families. Boys came into the police stations saying: "Charge me with vagrancy or anything, but don't send me out there!" pointing to the streets where other boys, as young as twelve and thirteen years of age were being beaten and stripped of their clothes. . . . Not more than half of the victims were actually wearing zoot-suits. A Negro defense worker, wearing a defense-plant identification badge on his work-clothes, was taken from a streetcar and one of his eyes was gouged out with a knife. Huge half-page photographs, showing Mexican boys stripped of their clothes, cowering on the pavements, often bleeding profusely, surrounded by jeering mobs of men and women, appeared in all the Los Angeles newspapers. . . .

At midnight on June seventh, the military authorities decided that the local police were completely unable or unwilling to handle the situation, despite the fact that a thousand reserve officers had been called up. The entire downtown area of Los Angeles was then declared "out of bounds" for military personnel. This order immediately slowed down the pace of the rioting. The moment the Military Police and Shore Patrol went into action, the rioting quieted down. On June eighth the city officials brought their heads up out of the sand, took a look around, and began issuing statements. The district attorney, Fred N. Howser, announced that the "situation is getting entirely out of hand," while Mayor Fletcher Bowron thought that "sooner or later it will blow over." The chief of police, taking a count of the Mexicans in jail, cheerfully proclaimed that "the situation has now cleared up." All agreed, however, that it was quite "a situation."

Unfortunately "the situation" had not cleared up; nor did it blow over. It began to spread to the suburbs where the rioting continued for two more days. When it finally stopped, the Eagle Rock *Advertiser* mournfully editorialized: "It is too bad the servicemen were called off before they were able to complete the job. . . . Most of the citizens of the city have been delighted with what has been going on." County Supervisor Roger Jessup told the newsmen: "All that is needed to end lawlessness is more of the same action as is being exercized by the servicemen!" While the district attorney of Ventura, an outlying county, jumped on the bandwagon with a statement to the effect that "zoot suits are an open indication of subversive character."

FURTHER INQUIRY

1. Do you think that the attitude of the press was partly responsible for the riot? Why?
2. What criticisms of the city officials' attitude can you offer?
3. What could the military officials have done?
4. Do you agree with the statement that "zoot suits are an open indication of subversive character"? Why or why not?
5. Is long hair also an indication of subversive character?
6. Could such incidents take place today? Why or why not?

The selection below provides further insight into the black protest movement. It was one of the earlier examples of resort to violent action on the part of the black community in Harlem. What factors may have encouraged departure from nonviolent protest?

10

Harlem Riot, 1964

by FRED FERRETTI *and*
MARTIN G. BERCK

THE new outbreak of violence was not as severe as the first rioting. It came minutes before the start of funeral services for James Powell, 15, the youth fatally shot by an off-duty white police lieutenant last Thursday, and less than 24 hours after the start of the worst rioting in Harlem since 1943.

From "Outbursts Snap Uneasy Truce—City's Leaders Ask for Calm and Restraint," by Fred Ferretti and Martin G. Berck, *New York Herald Tribune*, July 20, 1964. Copyright © 1964 by *New York Herald Tribune*. Reprinted by permission of *World Journal Tribune*.

The new rioting, in which four Negroes were shot by police, followed a day of efforts by ministers, community leaders and city officials to stem the anger of the country's largest Negro community. During the day Acting Mayor Paul Screvane urged the city's residents to "help maintain calm."

Only three hours before last night's incidents began, shortly before 5 p.m., Harlem Rent Strike leader Jesse Gray had asked an audience—which roared its approval—for "100 dedicated men who are ready to die for Negro equality."

As 150 persons crowded into the Levy and Delaney Funeral Home, 2250 Seventh Ave. at 132nd St., police manned barricades outside. About 200 steel-helmeted police, walking the center mall of Seventh Ave. began to duck scores of whiskey and milk bottles flung upon them from rooftops.

Revolvers were drawn and a volley of shots were aimed at the rooftops. The bottle-throwing stopped. Minutes later, however, the bottle barrage again started. Again police fired warning shots. The pattern continued sporadically.

During the day, some 400 police patrolled the debris-strewn sidewalks of Lenox, Seventh and Eighth Avenues between 125th and 139th Streets, where, in yesterday's early morning darkness, scores of pitched and running battles raged between police and groups of Negroes.

The resumption of street battling that came with darkness last night subsided gradually, and by midnight a police spokesman said the tension had "eased visibly."

Fifteen persons were shot, one fatally, and 116 injured, including 12 policemen, in the 12 hours of violence that followed three street rallies protesting the shooting of young Powell by Lt. Thomas Gilligan.

All four of the victims of last night's shootings were hit while police were scattering gangs. . . .

·   ·   ·

In Harlem's churches, impassioned pleas were made for an end to strife. A statement by Police Commissioner Michael J. Murphy urging "calm, lawful action" was read.

Civil rights officials conferred throughout the day and urged Harlem residents to stay off the streets.

Policemen were kept overtime at the riot scene and beefed-up patrols began at dusk.

Harlem shopkeepers swept up shattered storefront glass and took inventory following looting.

Another rally was planned for today, the day James Powell is to be buried. Mr. Farmer, national director of CORE, demanded that Mayor Wagner

Mimicry of "the white master" is no longer the criterion in black communities and the colorful garb of their African ancestors is worn more and more as a sign of independence. (Leonard Freed, Magnum)

return home from Spain. He also urged that Lt. Gilligan, who shot young Powell, be arrested "on suspicion of murder."

Bayard Rustin, who was jeered at the Jesse Gray rally, was hooted in the streets last night in front of the funeral home as he made repeated attempts to calm a crowd of angry Negro teen-agers.

Mr. Rustin and Rev. Milton A. Galamison, both of whom engineered the first city school boycott, had attended the funeral services and listened to the Rev. Theodore Kerrison of St. Augustine Baptist Church, 469 W. 148th St., deliver a low-keyed eulogy to young Powell.

"Death has to come to us all sooner or later," said Rev. Kerrison. He read the 23rd Psalm and as he was saying ". . . though I walk through the valley of the shadow of death . . ." a volley of shots rang out, intermixed with the crash of breaking bottles.

Mrs. Annie Powell, the dead boy's mother, was near collapse and sobbed hysterically as she was led from the funeral parlor into a waiting auto.

As the family left, a sound truck drew up in front of the funeral parlor. Mr. Rustin entered the truck to speak to the restive crowd.

"I urge you to go home. We know there has been an injustice done. The thing we need to do most is respect this woman whose son was shot." The crowd shouted "Uncle Tom Tom Uncle Tom." . . .

Mr. Farmer said he spent the night on the streets in the midst of the violence. Yesterday he said, "I saw a bloodbath. I saw with my own eyes violence, a bloody orgy of police . . . a woman climbing into a taxi and indiscriminately shot in the groin . . . police charging into a grocery store and indiscriminately swinging clubs . . . police shooting into tenement windows and into the Theresa Hotel. I entered the hotel and saw bullet holes in the walls . . .

Commissioner Murphy said, . . . "Some persons have used this unfortunate incident (the Powell shooting) as an excuse for looting and vicious, unprovoked attacks against police. In our estimation this is a crime problem and not a social problem." . . .

FURTHER INQUIRY

1. Do you feel that the crowd was justified in calling Mr. Rustin "Uncle Tom"? Why do you think they called him this?
2. Do you agree with Commissioner Murphy's statement that the riot "is a crime problem and not a social problem"?
3. Is looting a necessary by-product of rioting? Why or why not?
4. Police are often charged with brutality. How would you distinguish between appropriate police action and brutality?
5. What was Mayor Wagner's responsibility during the riot? What are the various ways in which mayors can act during riots?
6. Why was an important civil rights leader like James Farmer unable to control the rioters?

Robert Conot's investigation led him to conclude that the 1965 Los Angeles riot "is a significant turning point in Negro-white relations in the United States," that it "symbolized the end of the era of Negro passivity," and that it "placed on record the fact that the Negro has become a power in the cities." Why did he say this?

In the selection below we read of a meeting in Athens Park at which the Negro community discusses its feelings of rage and frustration with life in general and with the government, police, and the mayor in particular. Present were the black residents and official and quasi-official organizations of the community.

11

The Meeting at Athens Park

by ROBERT CONOT

THE gripes of the Negro community, both relevant and not, now started bouncing freely through the room.

"Who's getting all that poverty money?" An irate woman jumped up. "Big deal politicians sittin' up there in city hall making $10,000, $15,000 a year,

From *Rivers of Blood, Years of Darkness* by Robert Conot (New York: Bantam Books, Inc., 1967), pp. 144–54. Copyright © 1967 by Bantam Books, Inc. Reprinted by permission of Bantam Books, Inc.

In the ghetto a $2 steak can cost $4. A 20¢ can of beans can cost 35¢ and common staples can double in price. Should the finger of guilt, in a true sense of justice, be pointed toward the proprietors or the looters? (Wide World)

and the poor peoples supposed to be gettin' a $1.25 an hour, and they won't even let us have that! Who's puttin' them moneys in their pockets, that's what we wants to know!"

"Amen!"

"You tell 'em, sister!"

"Big fat Mr. Charley, that's who's gettin' it!"

The antipoverty program in Los Angeles had been caught in a classic political snarl. Although the city had been the first funded under the legislation, and $5 million had been allocated by the end of 1964, a dispute had arisen in the spring of 1965 between Mayor Sam Yorty and community agencies regarding the makeup of the governing board. . . .

"Why don't Yorty never come down here? The way he treat us, Watts might as well be in Birmingham!"

"He worse than Birmingham! In Birmingham, the mayor at least come down and see how the soul folk live."

It was true. The mayor had not visited the southeast area since his election. He had been elected the first time largely as a result of the Negro vote, but he was now blaming "Communist agitation" for every Negro demand.

"When we gonna get jobs? How we gonna live if we got no jobs?"

"How we gonna get jobs when the police keep harassing us, so we gets a record and *the man* won't give us no job?"

"Like I was downtown yesterday all day at the state employment office, and I come back last night, and the police grabs me and push me up against the wall, and ask me what I doing and all sorts of silly questions, and then they write up this little piece of paper on me and let me go! Next time I try to get a job, the man gonna say I have a record. So what's the use?"

(The youth had no record. Police had merely filled out a *field intelligence report,* which never passes beyond the local station and is destroyed after a period of time. However, since he *believed* he had been given a record, that belief tended to have more importance than the fact.)

.   .   .

For many years Los Angeles had had a peculiar ordinance, which made it a crime to file a false complaint against a police officer. In one such case a Negro waitress, getting off work and returning home at two o'clock in the morning, was stopped by a white motorist who attempted to rape her. Able to run to a nearby house, she called the police, who, refusing to believe her, had arrested her instead. When she subsequently registered a complaint against the officers, it was disallowed, and she was arrested again, this time for filing a false complaint.

Courts had ruled the ordinance unconstitutional in the early 1960's, but its effect lingers on, especially in the minority communities, where citizens feel that it is not only useless to make a complaint, since, in their view, all police officers are brothers-under-the-skin, but dangerous to themselves as well, since officers henceforth will be out to "get them." Aggravating the situation is the fact that the police department—unlike the sheriff's, which sends the complainant a full report regarding the disposition of the case—investigates the complaint and chastises the officer if it appears warranted, but never informs the complaining citizen whether his complaint was sustained or not—the effect being that the citizen, no matter what the disposition, is left to believe nothing was done.

It is this monolithic* face that the police department feels it must present to the world, so as not to lose the confidence of the average citizen, that infuriates the Negro, who time and again, personally and through friends, comes into contact with discourtesy and what he feels are unjust and arbitrary actions.

On the one hand, Chief Parker said, in a relatively secluded atmosphere,† "I never said there is no brutality. I can't belie my own figures." Figures that show that, over the span of the last 15 years, an average of about 25 officers per year have been separated from the department because of serious offenses. This 25 is an infinitesimal .5 per cent of the 5,000-man force, and, in this context, may be taken as a reassuring indication of the over-all excellence of the Los Angeles police.

On the other hand, considering that Parker himself stated that "it's what a man does at three o'clock in the morning [when there's no one else around] that makes or breaks the force," that each officer separated had a number of years of service at the time of separation, that there may be 100 rotten eggs on the force at any one time, and that each of these works 40 hours a week during which time he may have as many as 100 individual contacts with citizens, it becomes clear that the damage wreaked by even a few officers over a period of time can reach incalculable proportions.

. . .

"Look at me!" said a man. "I'm 40 years old, and I fought for my country, and I got a German bullet in me, and I come home, and they say to me, 'White people to the right, niggers to the left!' I'm the bot-

_____

monolithic—(literally—one stone), unchangeable.

† The McCone Commission hearings.

tom man on the totem pole, the last chicken in the pecking order. A few years back, I'm trying to get a job, me, an American who fought for his country, and next to me is a fellow who, it turns out, was a Nazi, and who do they give the job to? The Nazi, because he's blond and blue-eyed. So now they bring in all these Cubans, because they say Castro's discriminating against them, and whose jobs the Cubans gonna get? The American Negroes', who're being sent to fight in Vietnam so they can come home and take the back seat on the bus! Well, man, the Vietnamese never done nothing to the American Negro! But if they want to send me to fight in Mississippi, I'll join up right now!"

There were calls of "Amen!" and "You tell 'em!"

"You treat people like dogs, you got to expect they're gonna bite sometimes!"

"I've got seven sons!" A woman, very emotional, stood up. "And I'd just as soon see them die on the streets of Watts as in Vietnam. But that's not the way to do it! We want our rights, but we don't want to have to fight the police for them!"

"That's right!" a youth said. "We don't want no riots. We don't want no fights. We want to dance tonight!"

"All we wants is that we get our story told, and get it told right! What we do last night, maybe it wasn't right. But ain't nobody come down here and listened to us before!"

One of the ministers had invited Rena Frye* to the

The arrest of the Frye family was considered one of the precipitating causes of the Watts riot. Rena, the mother, was charged with interfering with an officer; Marquette, one of her sons, with drunken driving; Ronald, another son, with battery.

meeting. She, Marquette, and Ronald had been taken to the Firestone sheriff's station the previous night after being transported from the scene of the arrest.

On the ride to the station there had been, according to allegations, a further altercation. Mrs. Frye had inquired, "Why am I going to jail?"

To which an officer had replied, "Because your mouth is too big!"

The precise sequence of subsequent events is vague, but during their course Mrs. Frye was slapped, an officer was kneed, and Ronald was punched on the nose.

.   .   .

Following a suggestion made by Jim Burks of the probation department, John Buggs met with Ralph Reese and two other youths in a closed meeting in a small back room. Buggs wanted them to contact various groups and gangs of kids, who were known to be preparing to riot, and to pass the word that there wasn't going to be any march. It was a delicate situation, because, if the youths felt that they were being asked to fink on their friends, they would rebel.

.   .   .

"Fine, Mr. Buggs," Reese said. "If you can get the police not starting something, we'll do our best to get the blood to cool it."

.   .   .

It was almost 4 o'clock when Buggs left Athens Park. There had been one or two isolated rock-throwing incidents shortly after noon, and here and there groups of a half dozen persons were standing about; but the area in general was quiet.

.   .   .

Buggs then telephoned Fisk to inquire what action had been taken by the police department on the suggestions he had made that morning. Fisk told him that the department had decided not to pull back its men from the area, but that they were not going to saturate it either. They had decided that they were going to patrol as if it were any other day.

"I've made a commitment." Buggs was upset. "I promised the kids that if they wouldn't start anything, the police would stay out. If they see that my promises don't mean anything, this is going to put me in a very bad light."

Fisk said that he was sorry; that he had not been party to the decisions that had been made.

"Then can't you put a Negro officer in every car?"

"No," responded Fisk. That wouldn't be possible either.

"You've blown it!" snapped Buggs.

FURTHER INQUIRY

1. To what extent do you believe Chief Parker's views and the actions of the police were responsible for the riot?
2. What other reasons can you give to explain why the Los Angeles riot took place?
3. Given a position of authority, what would you do to prevent future riots in Watts and elsewhere?
4. Compare this selection with *Prelude to Riot* (p. 60). In what way do they deal with similar conditions?

Hostility and conflict have existed between the police and the black community of Detroit for a very long time. An episode occurred in the Algiers Motel during the July 1967 riot in which three black youths were killed and two white girls severely beaten. Pulitzer Prize winner John Hersey conducted a personal investigation. In the selection below, citizens of Detroit express their feelings about the riot, looting, and so on.

12

Echoes and Afterthoughts

by JOHN HERSEY

Trying to Get Something Free

AT first Lee and Sortor denied that they or their friends had done any looting. I was a more or less official-looking white person, and they had too long a habit of awareness that anything they said might

From *The Algiers Motel Incident* by John Hersey (New York: Bantam Books, Inc., 1968. Published by arrangement with Alfred A. Knopf, Inc.), pp. 59–62, 138–40. Copyright © 1968 by John Hersey. Reprinted by permission of Bantam Books, Inc.

be used to punish them to talk openly about the first phase of the riot. Like Michael toying with the lawyer in court, they put me on.

There apparently was, on that first day, a feeling of unwonted elation among those who ran in the streets. An articulate young black nationalist whom I met, a student at Wayne State University with a bright, fluid mind, told me, poking at the nosepiece of his horn-rimmed glasses to push them into place, fingering the tuft of beard under his lip: "There was a new thing, a new feeling, out there on Twelfth Street. I was out there Sunday. It was between noon and two o'clock that the feeling changed. After all those years of having the man in control—Detroit's an affluent town, Detroit's black people are well off—not middle-class, not even lower-middle, but upper-proletariat, I mean a cat can finish high school and get a job at a factory and buy a Pontiac and ride around and all, but the man has his finger on you every minute of every day. I mean, 'Show up at *this* time,' and, 'Do *this* on the assembly line,' and every minute of the day it's been what *he*'s said. And you get home, and the man is your landlord, and so on and so on. But out there, there was suddenly a realization. Man, the whole thing was *reversed*."

Another young militant at Wayne State, a girl with a carefully groomed natural hairdo, who talked with what seemed to be great honesty about black revolutionary ideology, hopes, and difficulties ("One trouble is—let's face it—we're all middle-class, and the hardest thing for us is to make contact with the folk—the real poor"), and about that first day: "On Twelfth Street everybody was out, the whole family, Mama, Papa, the kids, it was like an outing. . . . The rebellion—it was all caused by the commercials.

I mean you saw all those things you'd never been able to get—go out and get 'em. Men's clothing, furniture, appliances, color TV. All that crummy TV glamour just hanging out there." She was not the only one I talked with in Detroit who regarded television as the opiate of the white masses and the *agent provocateur* of the black masses. Some years before, watching TV along with most of the eleven children of the black farmer I was visiting in Holmes County, Mississippi, I had seen how, to the poorer blacks, the lily-white commercials act as an ironic affront and, even more, an ironic encouragement to violence. On the shows gunfire is commonplace, and what is more, it is necessary; it sells products. Virtue triumphs but the outlaw is mighty attractive—every day, every hour, he is sanctioned by the pretty white girl in the commercial lighting up and taking a deep puff as a preliminary to romance, or caring about her soft hands even when washing the dishes, or naked in the shower behind the ripple glass, arms raised to the white, white lather in her blond, blond hair.

"I thought it was real ridiculous," Thelma Pollard, Auburey's sixteen-year-old sister, said to me. "I wouldn't call it a riot. When it first started off I'd just call it everybody trying to get something for nothing, you know, because everybody was just breaking in and stealing things, trying to get something free. That's the way I thought it was."

Trans-Action quoted an unnamed youth, who was in the main part of the Algiers on the night of the shootings, on Sunday's looting: "I heard a friend of mine say, 'Hey, they rioting up on Twelfth!' I said what are they doing and he said looting. That's all it took me to get out of the house. He said the police was letting them take it; they wasn't stopping it; so I said it was time for me to get some of these diamonds and watches and rings. . . . People . . . were trying to get all they could get. They got diamonds here, they got money here, they got clothes here and TV's and whatnot. What could they do with it when they bring it out except sell it to each other? That's all. They're just getting something they haven't got. I mean, I bought me some clothes from somebody. I have exchanged whiskey and different things for different things. You know, something I wanted that I didn't have. This was a good way to get it. I really enjoyed myself."

Mr. Gill, when he told me about that Sunday afternoon, played down the joy. "I was laying down," he said. "It was about five thirty, I'd been down about twenty-five minutes, and I was just dozing. Someone unlatched the door. . . . I said, 'Where'd you get that?' Carl said, 'Oh, they're rioting, they're rioting.' So Carl and them got ready to go out, and I said, 'Man, don't go out,' I said, 'because somebody's going to have to pay for this. They're not going to let you just get away with it.' I kept telling them, man. I don't think they enjoyed it, because everybody was scared. Most of the people I met, they were just doing it, but they still had this fear." There was undoubtedly a generational gap in the experiencing of pleasure in the uprising and, indeed, in the looting itself. Of the 7,231 persons arrested altogether in the riot, 4,683, or just about two out of three, were between the ages of sixteen and twenty-eight, and only 981, or 13.5 per cent, were over forty.

Several months after the riot the boys began to relax and open up. Sortor murmured to me one day, "Sure. We was doing a bit of looting." Some days

Is the expression on this looter's face brought about by her destructive blow dealt to the system or by the bottles

later he said that the friends had looted some clothing from a store on Grand River and they had also looted some food, but Punkin and Melvin put it in their car and took it home. Another day he said, "Me and Auburey got a couple radios, me and him went down, then he went on home. We sold them. Different people down the street, they'd buy them. You just be walking down the street, or you'd either be sitting up there, and somebody say, 'You selling that radio, man?' You say, 'Yeah, yeah, I'm selling

in hand that will enable her to escape for a short time from the confines of her dismal world?

it.' 'I'll pay you so-and-so for it.' 'Okay.' We got fifteen dollars for them."

"Auburey came back home, you know," Thelma said to me, "he came back and he said he seen this box sitting in the street and he picked it up. My mother told him to don't be picking up that stuff and be carrying it home. He was scared and he thought somebody might have seen him picking it up and he took it back down and he came on back home. And he sat home the rest of Sunday looking at

149

television because he was scared to go out. You know, he'd get scared if he'd find out he was going to die or something like that, you know. My momma said they'd kill everybody, so he stayed home."

Everybody's Taking Everything

Charles Moore, a forty-one-year-old shear operator at Rockwell Standard who told me that he earned $15,000 last year and that his wife earned $10,000, lived in a predominantly white middle-class neighborhood in northwest Detroit, near Oak Park. He had been suffering from a coronary insufficiency and had arranged to enter Ford Hospital the following Saturday for some tests. (The day I first met him, some time after the riots, Moore was an indignant father, shaking his head over "today's kids." He said he had entered his two daughters, Jane, who was in ninth grade, and Barbara, in fourth, in a private school, mostly for white children, called Lutheran West, and was paying $600 a year tuition "to help them get something better than I've had." Moore, a quick-tongued man, had experienced among other difficulties in two decades no less than thirty-three arrests, sixteen of them for traffic violations and most of the rest for quarrels of one kind or another. Just the day before, he had been telephoned by a store called Allington's in the neighborhood and had been told that Jane was being held by the store; she had pilfered some hair curlers. He went and got her—charges were not pressed—and asked her why, *why*. She said, "I just want to be like the other kids, Daddy. They said I was trying to be elite"—she pronounced it *ee-light*—"because I wouldn't steal, and because I go to school with white kids." During the riot, he said, one of the girls had said to him, "Everybody's taking everything. What did you get, Daddy?" "They seem to think," he said, "that there's some kind of prestige in it, or something—take because everybody else is taking!")

That Sunday Charlie Moore drove in his '66 Cadillac across the river to Canada with two friends, James and Norah Adams, who were staying in room 14 in the main part of the Algiers Motel. During the day they had heard about the riot on the radio, and coming back they were searched at the bridge. Driving up Woodward Avenue, Moore stopped at a red light and was waiting for the light to change. Two police scout cars were directly in front of him. The driver of the one nearest him, a policeman, jumped out, apparently to chase a looter. The car started backing up, and it ran right into Moore's car. Moore had vainly blown his horn. Immediately after hitting the Cadillac the scout car shot forward and plowed into the other scout car; then it backed up again and came back at a higher speed and hit Moore's car again.

"See, what had happened," Moore explained to me, "when the driver jumped out he reached up to the gearshift level to put his car in neutral but he put it in reverse instead and ran off and didn't notice. Then a state trooper sitting in the back, see—they were working mixed teams, city police and state police—he reached forward to put it in neutral, but just then they hit me and it jogged him so he put it in forward, see. And then the very same thing happened at the other end of the line, only the other way around, so wham! I got it again. We had quite some discussion. They had to tow away the rammer there —a City of Detroit car. James and Norah took a cab on to the Algiers. The disturbance was going on all around us, and while we were arguing there, the man heard a brick go through some glass and just jumped in his car and took off with my license! Man! I had to report a lost license at the First Precinct, see. I didn't want to get caught without a license in the middle of a riot. By the time I finally got to the Algiers, James and Norah weren't there, they had went to her sister's."

FURTHER INQUIRY

1. Why do the blacks feel that television encourages violence? Do you agree?
2. "Of the 7,231 persons arrested about two out of three were between the ages of sixteen and twenty-eight." How do you account for the fact that so few persons over forty participated in the rioting and looting?
3. Why did the riot take place in Detroit, a city that had a large, black middle class? What does this indicate about riots?
4. Why did Jane Moore take part in the looting? What feelings exist between the middle-class and poor blacks?
5. How can knowing about riots of the past prevent future ones?

A few hours after the death of Dr. Martin Luther King, Jr., on April 4, 1968, destruction, death, fires, looting, and rioting broke out in the nation's capital. For years the citizens, black and white, believed that the city was riotproof because many blacks had secure government jobs. How do you account for this attitude when some of the worst slums of the nation are in the capital?

13

"All You Need Is a Match, Man"

by BEN W. GILBERT *and*
THE STAFF OF
The Washington Post

A FEW days after the occupation of Washington ended, *The Washington Post* assigned a reporter to find and interview some arsonists. . . . He began at once making contact with persons who might lead him to someone who would talk. At first, he was told that anyone who set fires would not agree to

From *Ten Blocks from the White House* by Ben W. Gilbert and the Staff of *The Washington Post* (New York: Frederick A. Praeger, Inc., 1968), pp. 156–64. Copyright © 1968, The Washington Post Company. Reprinted by permission of Frederick A. Praeger, Inc.

talk for publication. He persisted, suggesting that the interview be conducted with the arsonists wearing masks or hoods so that their identities would not be known. For nearly four months, there was no response.

Then, on August 8, around noon, the telephone rang.

"About the meeting. Do you still want it?"

When the reporter said "yes," he was told to expect another call around 10:00 P.M.

At 10:15 P.M., the same voice on the telephone told him to appear in front of a specified room in a shabby old hotel, in the heart of Washington's inner city. The reporter, who is black, said he would like to have another reporter accompany him.

"No, we don't want anybody else. Just you."

Armed with a tape recorder, the reporter appeared alone at the hotel room and knocked on the door. After he identified himself, he was made to wait two minutes. Then the door opened just a crack. A pair of eyes peered at him from two small holes in a black hood and he was allowed to enter.

The only light came from a lamp on the floor of an open closet. It cast a dull, eerie glow on three hooded figures in the small room. One was the black-hooded man who had opened the door. The other two wore improvised hoods, made from white hotel linen, with jagged holes torn out for eyes and mouths. One had also covered himself with a bedsheet, from his neck to his shoes.

Ground rules for the interview were quickly established. . . . The trio balked at the idea of using a tape recorder, but agreed when the reporter promised to destroy the tape after the interview was transcribed. . . . However, as the interview progressed, they began to warm up to the tape recorder and even orated into it. (The tape was destroyed as soon as the transcript was made.)

The interview proceeded for an hour and forty minutes. . . . One man had a .45 caliber automatic in his belt. Once, hearing a noise in the hallway outside the room, he nervously drew it. . . .

The purpose of the interview was to learn about arson in the April riot, but, as the session went on, it became evident that the three men were purporting to describe an unknown aspect of the riot—the fact that a small group of revolutionary activists had worked to keep it going.

The three made no claim that they or their group were responsible for starting the disorder in Washington. . . .

They did claim, however, to have performed a catalytic* role in the riot, by example and suggestion.

"A lot of areas we went into, man, there was nothing going on till we got there," one of them said.

The scope of their activity was limited, they said, by the relatively small size of their group and because Dr. King's assassination caught them by surprise. They took strong exception to the word "riot," preferring "rebellion" or "revolution" instead. They did not see what happened in Washington as a reaction to Dr. King's murder as much as an assault on a racist system, which, they believe, must be destroyed if black Americans are to survive.

The reporter felt that their basic story, told four months after the events of early April, was not inconsistent with what was known. This, too, was the judgment of senior reporters and editors who listened to the tape and examined the unedited transcript. It was decided that the interview should be published to

---

catalytic—causing action.

help in understanding the reactions and attitudes held by some participants in the riot. The transcript was then edited for space and clarity, with less relevant portions omitted.

The reporter assigned numbers to the three men, who had spoken to him as follows:

No. 1: I guess what you want to hear about is what happened after Dr. King got killed. Right?

REPORTER: Right. But specifically about burning.

No. 1: We've had ourselves somewhat organized in this city alone, I'd say, since about February. We felt for quite some time that it has been necessary to protect ourselves, to arm ourselves, in case the beast does decide to come down on us. . . . We had some of our equipment at close hand, where we could get to it easily, even with the curfew being in effect.

REPORTER: When you say equipment, what do you mean?

No. 1: Cocktails, even dynamite. There were a couple of places in this town that were dynamited. A&P at Benning Road, Cavalier's on 7th Street, were dynamited, and a couple of other places. But to get to burnings and things. We were preparing to make our own move with the slightest motivation, with the slightest incident that we could use to move with. We had the reason, but, in order to move, you must have the people behind you, also.

REPORTER: You used Dr. King's murder as an excuse?

No. 1: That's not the wording I used, brother man. I said we needed an incident that would make it justifiable even in the eyesight of the mass of the people that do not agree with the term "black power." With the mass of people that do not agree with protecting oneself with a piece [gun] such as

I have on my side, you see. We had some people who still think that the white man is a good man and he will set us free. Jesus with blue eyes and blond hair. I see the white man as a beast, not only from anybody's terminology but from my own past experiences. I was raised in the South, man; I've dug on it there, you see. . . .

REPORTER: What was the first place you burned? Or threw a bomb?

No. 1: The first place that I personally burned? My first thing I did was not the part of burning, as such. I believe in a total type thing. So I just stuck the cap on, lit it, and threw it, you know.

REPORTER: You put the cap on what?

No. 1: On a stick of 'mite.

REPORTER: Where?

No. 1: A&P. . . .

REPORTER: How did you obtain the dynamite?

No. 3: Well, like in Maryland and Virginia, they have sites where they keep dynamite. . . .

REPORTER: It was stolen from there?

No. 3: It was liberated.

REPORTER: Where did you learn to make Molotov cocktails?

No. 1: I learned in the service. Uncle Sam taught me in Army basic training. . . .

REPORTER: Why did you use fire after Dr. King was killed?

No. 3: I think what you're trying to say—why did you use fire instead of bullets?

No. 2: Because fire is more destructive, and it's much faster to destroy a building or the contents of most of the buildings with fire than any other means other than dynamite, and we had a limited amount of that. We had to hit special places with that.

REPORTER: Why were they special places?

No. 2: Well, because, first of all, like they were the biggest Jews and the biggest exploiters in the community, and we wanted to make sure they never did get back.

REPORTER: Why do you want to destroy in the first place?

No. 3: First of all, fire is the only thing that people could identify with. People are not ready for an

No compromise is the cry echoed by urban blacks who, feeling powerless and enraged, bring their grievances into the streets. (Free Press, Black Star)

armed thing right now. And we were not ready either—for an armed thing. We had been preparing for both fire and guns, but we didn't have enough and we didn't feel the people had enough guns. We knew the pulse of the whole city, because we worked in it, we've lived in it, you know, we were block workers and everything. And, like, twenty-five of us knew that it wasn't time for that. . . .

REPORTER: Did the fact that the police didn't shoot generally have any influence on your not using guns?

No. 3: No. If they had shot more, we would have just kinda come on out, you know, for the protection of our people. But since they didn't use them, we had decided not to use them. We had said we weren't going to do this thing all the way. But we decided in the beginning, too many black people would get killed for our mistake—for our not being ready.

REPORTER: There were seven people who died in fires. Does the fact that they died bother you? And they were blacks.

No. 3: No. I hate to see them go, but I came to the conclusion and to understand black people are going to have to die. . . .

REPORTER: What went through your mind as you were burning the place? Did you get any satisfaction from doing it? Were you avenging Dr. King's death, or what?

No. 2: My thing wasn't because of Dr. King's death, to me, personally, you know. Yeah, I got a satisfaction. As long as I can destroy the beast in any form I can—you know, economically, physically or any other form. But I have to wait my time.

REPORTER: The beast? Meaning who?

No. 2: The honkie, the whiteys. . . .

REPORTER: Where do you get this word "beast"? Is that just the latest thing for honkie?

No. 1: Well, it's not the latest thing. It is not a faddish word. It's a description, man, it's a reality. He is a beast. If you dig on his history you see he has done beastly things all his time. I mean, he walks different, smells different. He's a beast, baby. It's quite that simple. I wasn't completely satisfied because the revolution wasn't into a full-scale thing, because our people didn't think it was time for a full thing. In other words, a lot of people are still, what I say, in the Negro state of mind. The Negro state of mind being that of loving the white man or thinking that the white man is not all bad. I got some satisfaction, because I was doing something to hurt him. I know he's an exploiter of our people. Even they recognize the fact. They'll put on the news that in some stores in the ghetto areas, on the day that the people receive their welfare checks, the prices are hiked two and three cents on each item, so they can make a better profit on poor people who are living on welfare as it is.

REPORTER: You want to destroy those stores?

No. 1: I personally want to destroy the system. . . . Dr. King, the king of love, got killed because he preached love for all, you dig it. . . .

FURTHER INQUIRY

1. Why were the men wearing masks?
2. Why were certain areas burned and not others?
3. Can rioting lead to revolution? How would you distinguish between the two?
4. Are riots planned? What part did the three men play in this riot?
5. Why was the white man called "the beast"?

The incidents in this selection are from a report submitted to the National Commission on the Causes and Prevention of Violence. On July 23, 1968, three white policemen and four black civilians were shot to death in Cleveland. It has been called an ambush by the police and an armed uprising by blacks. This was the first time in urban violence that heavily armed blacks engaged in guerrilla warfare.

14

Reaction: The Crowds, the Police, and City Hall

by CIVIL VIOLENCE
     RESEARCH CENTER

TAKE an army of policemen, especially white policemen, into the ghetto, add a crowd of onlookers, and you have created a situation ripe for mass violence.

Just north of the Glenville battlefield lay Superior Avenue, a broad thoroughfare that carries U.S. routes

From *Shoot-Out in Cleveland* by the Civil Violence Research Center, Case Western Reserve University (New York: Bantam Books, Inc., 1969), pp. 55–58, 63–67. Copyright © 1969 by The New York Times Company. Reprinted by permission of The New York Times Company.

6 and 20. A crowd began to gather on Superior soon after the shooting started, barely within eyesight range of the shooting on Lakeview Road. The crowd became unruly, heaving rocks at passing cars and jeering at the police swarming into the area. When the body of a dead or dying sniper was carried toward the intersection, the smoldering hatreds of the crowd were aroused. "Look what they've done to one of our brothers!" some were heard to say.

By 9:30 P.M., the crowd had grown huge. Most in the crowd were young; by one estimate, the average age was twenty-two or twenty-three. Their mood was clearly hostile. "The crowd was berserk," one eyewitness recalls, and the police were frightened; they ran from their cars "like scared jack rabbits." A police car on Superior was hit by a Molotov cocktail; there was a "whoosh" and it went up in flames. The crowd scattered when ammunition in the car began to explode. A panel truck came down Superior and turned wildly directly into the crowd. The white driver was grabbed, pulled from the truck, and beaten to bloodiness. The crowd turned the truck over and set it afire. Herbert Reed, a 21-year-old patrolman, was pulled from his car at East 124th and Superior by a gang of Negro youths and beaten savagely. Two news cars containing valuable equipment were set afire and destroyed.

As they had done on the first night of the Hough riot* in 1966, the police sensed that the crowd was beyond control and they abandoned the situation. As the huge crowd began to move it found itself free of police restraint. A few black policemen remained to prevent cars with white occupants from running the Superior Avenue gantlet.

Hough—Cleveland's black ghetto.

Mobs began to spread along Superior. Teen-agers wrapped sweaters around their elbows and rammed plate glass windows of stores along the avenue, breaking them with a single thrust. "All you could hear was glass breaking," an eyewitness recalls. Gangs of looters and arsonists spread westward almost to Rockefeller Park, a buffer zone a mile away from Lakeview. At East 105th and Superior, close to Rockefeller Park, a block of buildings was burned to the ground. A store that Ahmed once had rented on Superior Avenue went up in flames, along with all the buildings next to it. Stores all along East 105th were looted. The violence spread all the way to St. Clair Avenue, more than a mile north of Superior. Sporadically it broke out on the other side of Rockefeller Park, as far west as East 55th Street and including the troubled area of Hough.

Patrol cars were dispatched to disperse looters, to answer calls of shootings, to pick up youths carrying gasoline cans or weapons. Often they had to report back "gone on arrival" or "unable to locate." A heavy rainstorm shortly after midnight offered hope of ending the violence, but the storm was short-lived. The looting and fire-setting continued through the night. Fire engines were brought in from all parts of the city and deployed in groups for protection against the hindering mobs. Firemen sometimes arrived on the scene to find hydrants had been opened, making it difficult to hook up hoses. They faced gangs of youths throwing bottles and rocks at them; some reported sniper fire. Eventually some fire crews refused to answer calls without a police escort. The next day Fire Chief William E. Barry reported that the Fire Department had responded to between fifty and sixty legitimate fires in the troubled area during the night, most of the fires occurring along Superior Avenue

Our laws of dissent permit a person to speak, to protest, to assemble peaceably. If the right to dissent is done with intent of injury to others or to property, the violator may be arrested and, if properly charged, convicted. (Wide World)

east of Rockefeller Park. About twenty were "major" fires, involving two or more buildings.*

Apart from those picked up as "suspicious persons" and those implicated in the Glenville shooting, twenty-eight Negroes were arrested during the night of July 23-24 in connection with the racial disturbances. Twenty-one were charged with looting, one with malicious destruction of property, two with burglary, and one with armed robbery. Three people related to one another were arrested near East 124th and Auburndale for carrying concealed weapons. All but five of the twenty-eight arrested were at least twenty years old. Five of those arrested were women.

·   ·   ·

Through the long night of July 23-24, 1968, Mayor Stokes and top officials at City Hall struggled with the decisions to be made about how to cope with the violence in Cleveland. They were hampered by inadequate and confusing information about the violence as it happened, and by the lack of contingency planning for such emergencies.

When he learned of the outbreak of shooting from Safety Director Joseph McManamon about 8:30 P.M., Stokes decided to meet with McManamon and others at Sixth District police headquarters, then changed his mind and moved the meeting to City Hall. When Stokes arrived at City Hall about 9 P.M., officials were monitoring the police radio and McManamon had a direct hookup for talking to police at the scene of the Glenville gun battle. The number

---

* Barry's figures were far in excess of those reported by others. In a summary report on the violence, issued August 9, the Mayor's office said there were twenty-four reported fires during the first twenty-four hours of violence, of which fourteen were set by vandals, one was a rekindle of an earlier fire, six were false alarms, and four were fires unrelated to the disturbance.

of patrol cars that had rushed to the Lakeview-Auburndale area, the tension of the situation there, the lack of coordination and measured response, made it difficult to assess what was happening. It was similarly difficult to get a clear picture of events as the violence spread. An aide described the situation at City Hall as "totally confusing."

.   .   .

Perhaps buoyed by its success after the assassination of Martin Luther King, the Stokes administration found itself inadequately prepared to handle the violence of July 23. Control of the situation was, in the beginning stages, left to police on the scene, and, as Stokes was later to admit, Cleveland police were inadequately trained and supplied to cope with urban guerrilla warfare.* According to Major General Sylvester DelCorso, Adjutant General of the Ohio National Guard, he had tried to get the Stokes administration to discuss measures for handling racial disturbances but had been rebuffed.

By 9:15 P.M., Stokes had decided that the situation might get beyond the control of local forces before the night was over. He called Governor James A. Rhodes, who was attending the National Governors Conference in Cincinnati, to inform him of the situation. The Governor immediately called General DelCorso, who was in Akron, and told him to report to Stokes. Within a few minutes, Rhodes left for his home in Columbus to monitor the disturbances from there, General DelCorso was on his way to Cleveland, and the Ohio National Guard had been placed on alert.

---

* In addition to lacking weapons equal in power to those the snipers used, the police lacked armored vehicles and had to commandeer trucks from Brinks, Inc. and rush them to the Lakeview area.

The signs of war. Not since Reconstruction days has so
much devastation shown its violent face. The black move-

ment is, in truth, a new civil war with new rules and no room for the gentleman's code. (Benedict J. Fernandez)

In addition to determining the level of force needed to control the violence, Mayor Stokes knew that he would have to inform the public of the situation, to avoid misunderstanding and panic and to keep people out of the troubled area. After talking to the Governor, the Mayor went down the street from City Hall to the television studios of WKYC. There he taped a special announcement to be used by WKYC and distributed in copy to other Cleveland television and radio stations. Many Clevelanders, watching a televised baseball game between the Cleveland Indians and the Baltimore Orioles, got the first news of the violence when Mayor Stokes interrupted the broadcast shortly before 11 P.M.:

> We've had a bad situation here tonight but as of this time we have the situation controlled. But we do need badly the help of every citizen at this time, particularly in the Lakeview-Superior Avenue areas. Stay at home and cooperate with the police. Go home if you are on the streets; if you are at home, stay inside and keep your doors locked so that we can contain the situation.

Later this message was broadcast over the Civil Defense network.

．　　．　　．

By 3 A.M., when Gen. DelCorso notified him that he had a number of troops ready for deployment, Mayor Stokes had decided that the time had come to use the National Guard. Two hundred Guardsmen, together with twenty-four jeeps and other military vehicles, were sent to the troubled area to patrol the streets. To each of the jeeps were assigned three Guardsmen and one Cleveland policeman. About 4:30 A.M. the police, on orders from the Mayor, were instructed to report any sniper activity to the National Guard. Looters and arsonists, said the police-radio announcement, "are to be arrested by police or National Guard without the use of deadly force." Half an hour later, the police heard another announcement on their patrol-car radios: All vacations and holidays are cancelled; all personnel will work twelve-hour shifts.

As dawn arrived amid a drizzle, smoke still rose from gutted buildings along Superior Avenue. Police continued to receive reports of looting and of sporadic gunfire in areas of the East Side. But the worst of the violence had abated. Cleveland, for the time being, was under control.

.   .   .

FURTHER INQUIRY

1. To what extent do you feel that Mayor Stokes' action helped to restore calm to the city? How did his decisions differ from those of other mayors in cities like New York and Los Angeles?
2. Why do you think that the shoot-out occurred in a city with a black mayor?
3. When is the use of the National Guard justified?
4. What are the advantages or disadvantages of increasing the number of black policemen in city police departments?

Anti-war demonstrators, innocent by-standers, newsmen, young, old, and the Chicago police battled in the streets of Chicago during the 1968 Democratic National Convention. This riot will be remembered in history as one of America's most shameful episodes. In Part A of the selection below journalist Jimmy Breslin documents the savagery of those days; in Part B, Chicago's Mayor Daley gives his defense of police tactics. These two views raise several questions: What happens to protest when the channels of dissent are blocked? Who or what was responsible for the chaos that took place?

15

A. "Kill the Body and the Head Dies"

by JIMMY BRESLIN

. . . IN Chicago, . . . the police . . . were everywhere. Full bellies pushing against the blue short-sleeved shirts. Round faces bulging under the helmets. The eyes wide open and burning.

"They don't represent my kids," an inspector says with a voice that is high with emotion. He is stand-

From *Telling It Like It Was: The Chicago Riots*, edited by Walter Schneir (New York: Signet Books, The New American Library, Inc., 1969), pp. 65–70. Copyright © 1969 by The New American Library, Inc.

ing on the sidewalk in front of the Conrad Hilton and pointing across to the crowd of young people in the park.

"They don't represent my kids," he says again. "Look at them . . . them . . . them . . . they all got scurvy, you touch them you get scurvy. They don't represent my kids. My kids are clean."

"They represent somebody," he was told.

"They shouldn't be in this town," he shouts. "The bastards."

"It's a political convention," he was told.

"They don't represent my kids!"

There was no way to talk. The cops had one thing on their mind. Club and then gas, club and then gas, club and then gas. In the afternoon, three of them, two in the back seat and one in the front, sat in a squad car parked on the drive which goes through the park that is across the street from the Conrad Hilton. . . . [T]he three of them wore black leather gloves. . . . There was something inside the gloves. The boxing people would call it a gimmick. Probably the gloves were lined with lead.

"What have you got gloves on for?" the cops were asked.

They shrugged. One of them smiled. "When you search people, they put glass and open knives in their pockets and you cut your hands when you search them," he said.

"Is that why?"

"Sure, how'd you like to get your hands cut?" he said.

The one sitting next to him began tapping his gloved hands together, getting the feel of whatever was inside them.

Late that night, very late, Katy Schefflein, 18, was

standing in the hallway outside the 11th floor night court in the Chicago Police Headquarters building. She is a slim girl who was in a sweater and slacks. Her right eye was half closed. The discoloring ran down to her cheek. A sheet of blood covered most of the surface of her eye.

"What happened to me, I ran into cops," she said.

"What did they hit you with?" she was asked.

"I don't know, I guess a fist," she said. "I don't remember seeing a club. I guess one of them just hit me with his fist."

Most cops, and most men anyplace, don't have the coordination and leverage to punch hard enough with their fists to do this to a person's eye, even a girl's eye. To make the blood come out into the eye the way it was in this girl's eye, and the blood will be there for weeks if I know my black eyes, to do this, you have to be an extraordinary puncher. Or you

Violence is not restricted to the black protest movement. Police action in Chicago erupted into a violence of its own and led to the passage of new laws that turned the handcuffs back upon those who chose to misuse them. (Roger Malloch, Magnum)

have to punch with a fist that is covered with black gloves that are gimmicked.

So these pigs in police uniforms punched and gassed and clubbed and I still don't know why they didn't shoot. Certainly, they wanted to. They were beside themselves. "Hey! Stop that!" an inspector shouted at three policemen beating a kid in the Conrad Hilton lobby. The cops did not stop clubbing the kid with these short chopping strokes to the kidneys and groin. They took no orders except from the wild thoughts which ran through their minds. The cops were at the Conrad Hilton Hotel in Chicago, but the Algiers Motel* never was far away.

And when the tear gas filled the air and slowly rose and came through the open windows of Hubert Humphrey's suite, the Vice President went into the shower.

Algiers Motel—see reading on p. 144.

Mrs. Jane Buchenholz, an elected McCarthy alternate from the West Side, sat in the back of the courtroom in the police station after she had been released on bond. She had spent five hours in jail cells and, delegate to a convention or not, she was stripped and searched twice for narcotics and knives and guns which, of course, she always carries. She had on a white knit suit and she was saying that the next time she would know enough to wear a dress that buttons down the front because then the matrons only unbutton you instead of making you take your clothes off.

"You know, I feel so sorry for Hubert Humphrey," she said. "I've known him for years. I feel sorry for what we made him do to himself. His ambition destroyed his soul. We let him do that to himself."

I felt sorry for the man, too, at first. If you ever have talked to Hubert Humphrey, you know that he understood and he had compassion and a great deal of natural sense. But in Chicago, with the smell of the White House so close to him, he turned into ectoplasm.* Most people were saying he was rice pudding. I don't have that much against rice pudding. Ectoplasm was a better name for Humphrey. It shouldn't have been this way. Once, he stood for so much.

I felt sorry for him until, the other night, I was sitting home and watching an interview Humphrey gave to Channel 13. It was a campaign interview. His eyes were alert and he was being very presidential and dignified and you could see him driving these points home; points he hoped would take him to the White House.

"Professional *agitat-ors,*" he said carefully. "The

---

ectoplasm—a formless substance.

language, it was horrendous . . . obscene and insulting to decent people, friends of mine . . . why these professional *agitat-ors* . . . what was Mayor Daley to do?"

.   .   .

The young people in front of the Conrad Hilton, these dirty, long-haired young, are the same kind of young people who passed out underground newspapers in Prague and shook their fists at Russian tanks. Hubert Humphrey, the old Humphrey, knows that. But the Humphrey of Chicago said to hell with that, I have my Law and Order issue. It is a weak Law and Order issue, not as good as the one Richard Nixon raises, but then Hubert Humphrey is only trying to catch up to Richard Nixon and he is not quite as artful at the game yet.

According to Humphrey, the city of Chicago was terribly hyped up by newspaper and FBI reports of throngs bent on disrupting the convention and assassinating all candidates and the Mayor of Chicago. On the newspapers, and television, he is correct. Yes, there was too much pre-convention publicity about possible violence. Far too much. But in the end, only 4,000 kids or so showed up at Chicago. . . .

Dick Fernandez was one of the professional agitators in the park across the street from the Conrad Hilton. He is from New York, and he is with Dave Dellinger and Sidney Peck and Abbie Hoffman and Tom Hayden and the others who look for Columbia Universities* to take place everywhere. During the afternoon before the worst night in Chicago, he sat on the hood of a car parked on the drive going through the park.

"They're conferring with the police now," he said.

Columbia University—see reading on p. 77.

"We'll see what's what."

"What do you want to do?" he was asked.

"We say we want to march to the Amphitheatre. I hope they tell us no. If they tell us it's all right for us to march, that's the worst thing that can happen. Hell, we're dead if they say we can march. Five or six miles of a march. This whole thing will fall apart."

Peck came up with a loudspeaker. "All right," he said, "we've spoken to the police. They said we cannot march to the Amphitheatre. And if we remain here we are considered to be obstructing traffic and unlawful and we will be cleared out after proper notice. They didn't say what proper notice meant. So I suggest you break into small groups and just leave the park and re-form elsewhere."

"That's it," Fernandez said. "They did it for us."

Stupidity made the night possible. A permit to march, an escorted guided march to an Amphitheatre they could not have reached, would have ended it all. But we were dealing with such deep stupidity and unawareness and so many hardened brain arteries and dying brain cells in Chicago that the trouble was insured.

The professional agitators were a handful. The number of decent kids was large. The cops proceeded to riot. The cops claimed things were being thrown at them. Over the day and night, if there were more than a few instances of urine in cups being splashed at police, and little balls with spikes in them being thrown out, nobody saw them, and Michigan Avenue was loaded with reporters who threw nothing and were being struck by policemen. A demonstration which should have been handled as if it weren't even there was turned into an international incident because the police rioted.

Nobody has ever accused a policeman of being a social genius. A policeman is a working man who takes a job that is essentially a lousy job. The working man takes this job because of the pension. So you have a man working a job simply because he wants to get a pension in 20 years. A man who does this is not happy or imaginative. Police as a rule are poorly read. At the same time, these unhappy working men are wearing uniforms and they have clubs and guns. This means they must be controlled. They cannot be expected, or allowed, to handle delicate political or social matters without tight, iron tight, supervision. Actually, it is a crime that they are expected to handle a social or political matter at all. It is the job of the political leaders. But the political leaders do nothing and in the end they hedge off all the trouble to a cop who makes $8,500 a year and has a wife and three kids at home. It is unfair to the police. Here in New York, Mayor Lindsay, with wiseness; looking at it now, with wiseness nobody ever thought he had; has assigned two people from his office, Sid Davidoff and Barry Gottehrer, to work with both the demonstrators and the police in an effort to keep Chicago out of New York. The old hacks, the old police hacks and the old political hacks like Frank O'Connor, screamed about this. The Patrolmen's Benevolent Association's John Cassese said his police were tired of these two kids and something was going to be done about it. Well, after Chicago, after these police, totally unsupervised by anything but their own emotions, went on this rampage, you could see what civilians from City Hall, Gottehrer and Davidoff, have meant to the City of New York in the last three years. Do away with them? Like hell. Get ten more of them.

B. Daley's Defense

by MAYOR RICHARD DALEY

ON behalf of the City of Chicago and its people and the Chicago Police Department I would like to issue this statement and I expect that in the sense of fair play it will be given the same kind of distribution on press, radio and television as the mob of rioters was given yesterday.

For weeks and months the press, radio and tele-

From *Protest: Man Against Society,* edited by Gregory Armstrong (New York: Bantam Books, 1969), pp. 154–55. Copyright © 1969 by Bantam Books, Inc. Reprinted by permission of Bantam Books, Inc.

vision across the nation have revealed the tactics and strategy that was to be carried on in Chicago during the convention week by groups of terrorists.

The intention of these terrorists was openly displayed. They repeatedly stated that they came to Chicago to disrupt the national political convention and to paralyze the city.

They came here equipped with caustics, with helmets and with their own brigade of medics. They had maps locating the hotels and the routes of buses for the guidance of terrorists from out of town.

To protect the delegates and the people of Chicago from this planned violence the city worked with the Secret Service, the Federal Bureau of Investigation, the Department of Justice and other agencies directly involved in the maintenance of law and order. In every instance the recommendations of both the Kerner and Austin reports were followed— to use manpower instead of firepower.

The newspapers stated specifically that the terrorists were planning to use those who were opposed to the present Viet Nam policy as a front for their violence. It was also pointed out that they would attempt to assault, harass and taunt the police into reacting before television cameras. Fifty-one policemen were injured. Sixty percent of those arrested did not live in Illinois.

In the last two days we have seen the strategy of these announced plans carried on in full and the whole purpose of the city and the law enforcement agencies distorted and twisted.

One can understand how those who deeply believe in their cause concerning Viet Nam would be deeply disappointed, but to vent their disappointment on the city and law enforcement agencies—that these dissenting groups and television could be used as a tool for their purposes of calculated disruption and riot, is inexcusable.

In the heat of emotion and riot some policemen may have over-reacted but to judge the entire police force by the alleged action of a few would be just as unfair as to judge our entire younger generation by the actions of this mob.

I would like to say here and now that this administration and the people of Chicago have never condoned brutality at any time but they will never permit a lawless violent group of terrorists to menace the lives of millions of people, destroy the purpose of this national political convention, and take over the streets of Chicago.

FURTHER INQUIRY

1. To what extent does Daley effectively defend himself?
2. Would you agree with Mr. Breslin's view that police cannot be trusted with delicate social situations?
3. How can we get better prepared police? What preparation should they have?
4. In your view, were the demonstrators professional agitators?
5. Is it possible to have a police riot? Is this what happened in Chicago?
6. Why did the city of Chicago prevent the protest marches from taking place? Could this trouble have been averted by issuing permits?
7. Why was Chicago chosen for the Democratic Convention?
8. Would the same thing have occurred in other cities?

Notes

**Suggestions for
Additional Reading**

Index

Notes

THE PROBLEM AND THE CHALLENGE

1. *Report of the National Advisory Commission on Civil Disorders* (New York: Bantam Books, 1968), p. 1.

2. A riot is where three or more actually do an unlawful act of violence, either with or without a common cause or quarrel—*Blackstone Commentaries,* p. 46.

3. Ben W. Gilbert and the Staff of *The Washington Post, Ten Blocks from the White House* (New York: Frederick A. Praeger, 1968), p. 18.

4. Robert N. McMurry, "Who Riots and Why," *Nation's Business,* October 1967, pp. 72–75.

5. "Man's Relations to Man—Violence: A Christian Reassessment," *Current,* May 1968, p. 21.

6. Executive Order 11365.

7. *Report of the National Advisory Commission on Civil Disorders,* op. cit., p. 10.

8. National Commission on the Causes and Prevention of Violence, *Progress Report to Lyndon B. Johnson,* January 9, 1969.

9. Arnold Martin, "The Campus Revolutions: One Is Black, One White," *The New York Times,* May 12, 1969, p. 51.

10. *Report of the National Advisory Commission on Civil Disorders,* op. cit., p. 207.

11. A. Philip Randolph, "The March on Washington Movement," *Black Protest,* edited by Joanne Grant (Greenwich, Conn.: Fawcett Publications, Inc., 1968), p. 245.

12. National Commission on the Causes and Prevention of Violence, "Statement on Campus Disorders," *The New York Times,* June 10, 1964, p. 30.

13. M. S. Handler, "Poll Finds Riots Are Effective in Changing Slum Conditions," *The New York Times,* December 16, 1968, p. 32.

14. John Herbers, "Cities' Riot Sites Remain Desolate," *The New York Times,* April 13, 1969, pp. 1, 58.

15. The Walker Report, *Rights in Conflict* (New York: Bantam Books, 1968), pp. 1, 3.

16. "A Warning on Student Disorders," *The New York Times,* editorial, April 4, 1969, pp. 1, 18.

17. H. D. Graham and T. R. Gurr, *Violence in America* (New York: Signet Books, The New American Library, 1969), p. 439. (Official Report of The National Commission on the Causes and Prevention of Violence, June 1969.)

Suggestions for Additional Reading

1. BERNSTEIN, SAUL, *Alternatives to Violence: Alienated Youth and Riots, Race and Poverty*. New York: Association Press, 1967. A discussion of the causes of violence and alienated youth of the ghettos with proposals for nonviolent approaches to racial and economic progress.

2. COHEN, J. and MURRAY, WILLIAM S., *Burn Baby Burn. The Los Angeles Race Riot, August 1965*. New York: Dutton, 1966. An analysis of the underlying causes of the violence in Watts.

3. GRAHAM, HUGH DAVIS and GURR, TED ROBERT, *Violence in America: Historical and Comparative Perspectives*. New York: Signet Books, The New American Library, Inc., 1969. Prepared for The President's Official Commission on the Causes and Prevention of Violence, this investigation studies the history of violence in American life from frontier to present day and suggests methods for dealing with the causes. Included are police brutality, labor protest, ghetto rioting, assassinations, campus rioting, and vigilantism.

4. SILBERMAN, CHARLES E., *Crisis in Black and White*. New York: Vintage Books, a Division of Random House, 1964. A definitive study of the Negro problem in American society.

5. SKOLNICK, JEROME H., *The Politics of Protest*. New York: Ballantine Books, Inc., 1969. This report deals with black militants, student riots, anti-war demonstrations, white racism, and the use of law enforcement officers as a repressive force against social change.

6. WALKER, DANIEL, *Rights in Conflict*. New York: Bantam Books, 1968. This report to The National Commission on the Causes and Prevention of Violence presents the facts behind the confrontation between the Chicago police and demonstrators during the Democratic National Convention.

7. WARREN, ROBERT P., *Who Speaks for the Negro?* New York: Random House, 1965. The problems of Negroes in the United States are discussed with Martin Luther King, Adam Clayton Powell, Malcolm X, and others.

Index